THE
DEE BRESTIN
BIBLE STUDY SERIES

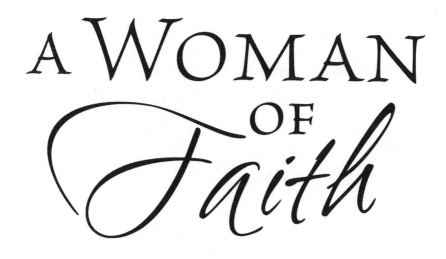

A WOMAN OF Faith

NEXGEN®

Building the New Generation of Believers

COOK COMMUNICATIONS MINISTRIES
Colorado Springs, Colorado • Paris, Ontario
KINGSWAY COMMUNICATIONS LTD
Eastbourne, England

The Dee Brestin Series
From Cook Communications Ministries
BOOKS

The Friendships of Women

The Friendships of Women Devotional Journal

We Are Sisters

We Are Sisters Devotional Journal

BIBLE STUDY GUIDES

A WOMAN OF LOVE
Using Our Gift for Intimacy (Ruth)

A WOMAN OF FAITH
Overcoming the World's Influences (Esther)

A WOMAN OF CONFIDENCE
Triumphing over Life's Trials (1 Peter)

A WOMAN OF PURPOSE
Walking with the Savior (Luke)

A WOMAN OF WORSHIP
Praying with Power (10 Psalms with a music CD)

A WOMAN OF HOSPITALITY
Loving the Biblical Approach (Topical)

A WOMAN OF MODERATION
Breaking the Chains of Poor Eating Habits (Topical)

A WOMAN OF CONTENTMENT
Insight into Life's Sorrows (Ecclesiastes)

A WOMAN OF BEAUTY
Becoming More Like Jesus (1, 2, 3 John)

A WOMAN OF WISDOM
God's Practical Advice for Living (Proverbs)

A WOMAN OF HEALTHY RELATIONSHIPS
Sisters, Mothers, Daughters, Friends (Topical)

THE FRIENDSHIPS OF WOMEN BIBLE
STUDY GUIDE correlates with
THE FRIENDSHIPS OF WOMEN

NexGen® is an imprint of
Cook Communications Ministries, Colorado Springs, CO 80918
Cook Communications, Paris, Ontario
Kingsway Communications, Eastbourne, England

A WOMAN OF FAITH
© 2006 by Dee Brestin

First printing, 2006
Printed in the United States of America
1 2 3 4 5 6 7 8 9 10 Printing/Year 10 09 08 07 06

Cover Design: Thinkpen Design, llc/Greg Jackson
Cover Photo: © 2006 Big Stock Photo
Interior Design: Nancy L. Haskins

ISBN: 978-0-7814-4448-4

Contents

To Kristen Wiebe,

who faces enormous danger daily

to be a vehicle of God's mercy

How I Thank God For:

Dr. John Bronson
Decades ago this wise pastor first opened my eyes to the text of Esther, helping me see beyond the "children's version" of this book to the empowering truth that can break the chains that bind us.

My editor,
Dorian Coover-Cox, who teaches Old Testament at Dallas Theological Seminary: You have inspired and encouraged me with your knowledge, discernment, and perspective.

The gifted team at Cook:
How beautifully you work together to bring glory to God.

To my late husband, Steve
I sense you are *still* praying for me and the women using this guide.

Introduction

As you read this introduction, underline or highlight any thoughts that have special meaning for you. In the first lesson you'll be asked to share these thoughts with the group.

My three daughters—and now my three granddaughters—love the story of Esther. I tell it to them with passion because I so want them to know that God hasn't limited them as women. Instead, He has uniquely gifted them to be able to enormously influence others for good.

As a parent, I wanted to tell my children the unedited version of Esther as soon as they were old enough to hear it. Too often, even as adults, we have a "children's version"—a "*Veggie Tales* version"—of Esther in our minds. But unless we examine every facet of this story and seek to understand the weaknesses and imperfections of the characters, the mistakes and compromises they made under pressure, and the reality of the sexual abuse that Esther and hundreds of other young women experienced, we won't be able to see the wonderful themes of repentance and redemption that follow.

Esther was one of the most breathtakingly beautiful women who ever lived, and her beauty was instrumental in helping to save her own life and the lives of the Jewish people. But if we look more closely at her story, we will see that Esther seemed to be defined by her beauty and by her ability to please the men in her life. The pressure she experienced was enormous, and in the beginning she succumbed to it by concealing her Jewish ancestry and taking part in the king's "beauty contest."

But there came a moment when Esther had to make a crucial choice. She could continue hiding her true identity, using her beauty to please the men in her life and doing only what was expected of her. Or she could choose to intercede for the lives of her people at great risk to her own life. As we'll see, by breaking free from those things that had defined her, Esther came into the identity and purpose for which she was born and went down in history as the woman who saved her people from a holocaust.

The book of Esther is one of the most challenging books to study because no editorial commentary is provided to help us evaluate the motives and actions of the characters in the story. God is strangely silent throughout the entire story. We can see His fingerprints if we look closely, but we never hear His voice or see clear evidence of His presence. In fact, Esther is the only book in the Bible in which God's name is never mentioned. In the absence of editorial commentary, we'll find ourselves pondering many difficult questions, such as: Why did Mordecai ask Esther to conceal her identity from the king? Why didn't he try to prevent her from being taken into the king's harem? Did Mordecai perhaps even ask her to participate in the king's "beauty contest," and if so, was he right to do so? Should Esther have refused to sleep with the king, or was she right to comply? What might have happened if Esther and Mordecai hadn't compromised but had instead determined to obey God? Why did Mordecai refuse to bow to the king's right-hand man, Haman, and was he right to do so? Was Vashti right to disobey her husband, and what was her motive? Did God's people, at the close of the story, go beyond waging a "just war" against their enemies to seeking vengeance? For example, when David committed adultery, we're told that "the thing David had done displeased the LORD" (2 Sam. 11:27). And when Miriam murmured in jealousy against her brother Moses, God not only rebuked her but also afflicted her with leprosy so that the whole camp would know of her sin (Num. 12:1–2, 10). But in Esther, God is silent (we'll consider the reasons for this later), leaving readers to wonder what conclusions they should make.

As you and the women in your group explore the story of Esther together, you will have many wonderful opportunities for lively discussions that will challenge and encourage you in your faith. I urge you to look deeply into the text, to pray for wisdom, and to be like the Bereans, who "were of more noble character than the Thessalonians, for they received the message with great eagerness and examined the Scriptures every day to see if what [they were being taught] was true" (Acts 17:11).

Despite God's silence throughout the story of Esther, despite the fact that His name isn't mentioned even once, His fingerprints are indeed everywhere. For this reason you'll also find it one of the most encouraging books you have ever studied. You'll not only see the weaknesses and failings of God's people, but you'll also find that in spite of everything, God cared for them, led them, and in the end, brought beauty out of ashes. When I think of all the mistakes I've made in my life, all the times I've failed Him, I'm so thankful for the redemptive message of the book of Esther.

As you work through this study, you'll also be stretched to become a "detective for the Divine," to see God's hand not only in the book of Esther but also in your everyday life. In the first lesson we'll look at the exciting theme of God's providence and how you can be more alert to His hand in your own life.

The book of Esther contains some particularly encouraging messages for women. While reading this story, I have heard my Heavenly Father say to women from every background and situation in life,

You live in a world that is much like ancient Persia, a world obsessed with wealth, youth, carnal entertainment, and sexual immorality. This world can squeeze you into its mold, affecting how you see yourself as a woman. I want to show you how much more I have for you than the world can ever give.

If you're a victim of sexual abuse, as Esther was, I want you to know that I grieve with you. For reasons you may not understand, I allowed it, but I never left you. I'm also a Master of bringing beauty out of ashes. I did it for Esther, and I can do it for you.

I created you uniquely as a woman. Because of the relational gifts I've given you, you can have an enormous impact on the men, women, and children in your life. You can either walk in the flesh as Haman's wife, Zeresh, did and reap destruction on your loved ones, or you can walk in the Spirit, as Esther learned to do, and bring salvation to your loved ones.

I can use you mightily as a woman. When Esther sought me, I gave her the wisdom and grace to overcome a king and his evil advisor and save her people from a holocaust. If you seek Me with your whole heart as Esther did, I will give you wisdom and grace to make a difference in your own family, church, and world. Listen carefully to Esther's story, look for My fingerprints, and see how I am able to bring beauty out of ashes.

Guidelines for Personal Study and Group Discussion

Just as God used Esther mightily to impact others, I'm praying that He will use you to impact the women in your small group as you seek to obey Him. Here are a few suggestions that will help you make a difference:

1. Do your homework at the same time and in the same place daily so that you'll establish a habit. *Expect* God to speak to you personally through His Word. Then when you meet with your group, it will be with an overflowing heart rather than an empty cup. What richness you'll experience together as sisters in Christ as a result! If you receive your guide just before your first small-group meeting and don't have time to complete the first lesson, I'd suggest working through the first two days as a group, reading the introductions and passages aloud together. Then assign the rest of the lesson as homework for the next week.

2. You'll notice that some of the questions in this study ask you to record your observations about the Scripture passage you've read, and others ask you to apply what you've learned. The observation questions form the critical foundation for the study, and if you don't observe the passage carefully, then your interpretation and application will be off base. Take your time and look, look, look.

3. If you don't already have a hymnal, I'd encourage you to buy or borrow one, because hymns will be suggested throughout this study to enrich your quiet time and help you prepare your heart for the day's lesson. You can use the Internet to find hymns, but it's often easier and faster if you have your own hymnal. (You'll also find a few well-known hymns in the back of this study guide.)

4. Be sensitive to others during your group discussions. Naturally talkative women need to exercise control and give others an opportunity to share. Shy women need to exercise faith and speak up more often. Follow Esther's example as you learn to discern when to speak and when to be silent.

5. Stay on target in your group discussions. Normally, these lessons can be discussed in ninety minutes. But if you don't have that much time, you have two options:

    A. Divide the lessons, doing two days the first week, and the remaining three the second. Do the prayer time both weeks. This will take you eighteen weeks.

    B. Do the whole week's lesson but discuss half the questions.

6. Follow the instructions for group prayer at the close of each lesson, making sure to keep all prayer requests confidential. When Esther and her maids fasted (and we assume, therefore, prayed), God worked mightily. There is power when women pray together.

7. A group is so much richer when women bond. Seek out opportunities to get to know the other women in your group by talking with them individually, e-mailing them encouraging thoughts, calling them during the week, inviting them over, sympathizing with those who are hurting, and simply sharing the love of Christ. You might also want to have a ladies' night out to share some of your best "Detective for the Divine" moments or to watch and discuss the movie *Esther* (available from my Web site, www.deebrestin.com).

One

"He Is There and He Is Not Silent"

Francis Schaeffer once said of God, "He is there and He is not silent."[1] Merrill Unger defined *providence* as "the continual care which God exercises over the universe which He has created."[2] God cares for all He has created, but especially evident is His providence toward His children.

Providence. Corrie ten Boom sensed it when she hid her Bible on her person, watched the guards at Ravensbruck thoroughly search everyone in line before and after her, and yet "happened" to walk through untouched.[3]

Providence. In a pasture in North Carolina, a group of men gathered to pray that "out of Charlotte the Lord would raise up someone to preach the Gospel to the ends of the earth."[4] That pasture "happened" to belong to Billy Graham's father.

Providence. Even though God isn't mentioned in the book of Esther, we can sense Him everywhere in everything that happens.

Often we don't understand the mysterious ways of God, and yet we can see the overwhelming evidence that He is there, that He cares, and that He has a plan for our lives that is good. When Joni Eareckson Tada was paralyzed in a diving accident, she cried out to the Lord, expressing the deepest, darkest questions of her soul. Did she receive an answer? Yes, an answer similar to the one Job received from God. And it came to her in the words of Romans 11:33–36:

> *Oh, the depth of the riches of the wisdom and knowledge of God!*
>
> *How unsearchable his judgments,*
>
> *and his paths beyond tracing out!*
>
> *"Who has known the mind of the Lord?*
>
> *Or who has been his counselor?"*
>
> *"Who has ever given to God, that God should repay him?"*
>
> *For from him and through him and to him are all things.*
>
> *To him be the glory forever! Amen.*

Joni said that if God *had* answered her questions more specifically, "it would have been like dumping a water tower into a Dixie cup. My poor pea brain wouldn't have been able to process it."[5]

God has *had* a plan from the foundation of the world, and He has never lost control. Your study of Esther will encourage your faith, for though it may seem as if God had lost control, He never had. In fact, what the prophets foretold about the events leading up to the story of Esther was fulfilled to the letter. This week's lesson will give you an overview of the book of Esther, the central theme of God's providence, the circumstances that led up to the events in the story, and the amazing fulfillment of prophecies that had been spoken more than a century earlier. It's always good to turn the puzzle box over and look at the big picture before you attempt to put the pieces together.

Prepare Your Heart to Hear

During this first week, you will not only read about the Old Testament prophecies that led up to the events in Esther, but you will also witness their fulfillment. Even though these prophecies may prove challenging to understand, they will provide you with important background information as you begin your study of Esther. So each day before you begin the lesson, ask God to help you understand what you're reading. He's eager to do so.

Memory Work

This week's memory verse is Romans 11:33, which provides a wonderful context for the book of Esther and will give you a richer understanding of the mysterious God who walks with you.

> *Oh, the depth of the riches of the wisdom and knowledge of God! How unsearchable his judgments, and his paths beyond tracing out!*

WARMUP

Introduce yourself and share why you're here. What are your hopes for this time?

DAY 1

A Detective for the Divine

Several times a week you will be a "Detective for the Divine" as you reflect on the various ways you've seen God at work in your life in the past twenty-four hours. The most typical ways to experience God are through the following:

A. HIS WORD

In what ways did God increase your understanding or love of Him today? Did He speak to a particular need in your life through the Scriptures you read? If so, how?

[HIS WORD]

B. HIS PRESENCE

In what ways did you experience God's presence today? He urges you to "be still, and know that [He is] God" (Ps. 46:10). When you do this, you're opening the drapes and allowing Him access to your life. He may come to you during your time with Him—when you're singing or listening to music or when you're simply asking Him to enter your world while you're taking a walk or having lunch with a friend. Be ready to be amazed!

[HIS PRESENCE]

C. HIS PROVISION

How has God provided for you today? This can be any blessing, as every good gift comes from God (see James 1:17). Jot down some of the gifts you're apt to take for granted, such as a sunset, a baby's smile, or good health. Or perhaps you've sensed unusual evidence of God's grace as we sense in the story of Esther. If so, what made you wonder whether God might be involved? Was a friend's e-mail particularly timely? Did different friends recommend the same book or tell you the same thing?

[HIS PROVISION]

1. What did you underline or highlight in the introduction to this guide? Briefly share why these thoughts had special meaning for you.

2. List three ways you can be a "detective for the Divine" each day.

Read Esther 1. (This overview is optional but strongly recommended.)

3. Briefly describe what happened in this opening chapter of Esther. (Watch for the satire, or you may miss the point.)

Detective for the Divine

How have you seen God at work in your life in the past twenty-four hours through the following?

A. His Word (What did you learn?)

B. His presence (When did you sense His presence?)

C. His provision (What did He provide?)

DAY 2
. . . .

God's People Are Taken Captive

One way we see the providence of God is through the Old Testament prophets. He used His prophets repeatedly to warn His people not to sin, telling them of the painful consequences that would result from a lack of obedience and genuine repentance. God was slow to anger in dealing with His people, and as Matthew Henry wrote, "We see the great pains that had been taken with the people to bring them to repentance."[6] However, despite the warnings, they persisted in sin, and as we'll see in today's Scripture reading, Jeremiah told them that God was going to carry out His threat to send them into captivity. This prophecy was fulfilled approximately 120 years before the story of Esther.

God's central purpose for our lives is to make us like Him, to help us become holy. How foolish we are when we trifle with the living God!

Read Jeremiah 25:1–14.

4. Answer the following questions based on your observations of the text.

A. How many years had Jeremiah warned the people about God's coming judgment? What was their response? (vv. 3–4)

B. What message had the prophets spoken to the people? What was the people's response? (vv. 5–7)

C. What two things does sin do? (v. 7)

D. Briefly describe some of the ways your sin has brought you harm.

More than a century before the events in the book of Esther occurred, the pagan king Nebuchadnezzar attacked and eventually destroyed Jerusalem, taking many Jews as captives to Babylon (see Dan. 1:1–7). Among them were Daniel, Shadrach, Meshach, Abednego, and Mordecai's great-grandfather Kish (see Est. 2:5–6; 2 Kings 24:8–16).

E. What would Nebuchadnezzar do to the Israelites and their land? List words and phrases that poignantly describe the loss to God's people. (vv. 9–11)

F. How long would it be before God punished Nebuchadnezzar for his sin? What would God do to the king and his nation? (vv. 12–14)

God can use unbelieving kings as His servants for His purposes. At this time in Israel's history, Nebuchadnezzar was an agent of God's wrath. Later, Cyrus would be an agent of His grace toward His people.

Read Daniel 1:1–8.

5. Answer the following questions based on your observations of the text.

A. How is Daniel 1:1 a fulfillment of Jeremiah's prophecy?

B. What request did the king make of the head of the palace staff? What kind of men did he want and for what purposes? (vv. 3–4)

C. Even when God's people are far from Him, He has always had a holy remnant. What were the names of the four men who were selected to enter the king's service? (Use their more familiar names, given to them by the chief official in verse 6.)

6. Read Esther 2:5–7 and trace the genealogy of Esther back to Kish, who had been one of the Jews taken into captivity along with Daniel.

Esther, cousin of Mordecai

Mordecai, son of _____

_____, son of _____

_____, son of Kish

Read Esther 2—3. (This overview is optional but strongly recommended.)

Summarize each of these chapters in a sentence or two.

Memory Work

Spend five minutes reviewing this week's memory verse. Often, memorizing a word at a time (ending with the Scripture reference) will help to cement it in your mind:

Oh,

Oh, the

Oh, the depth

Oh, the depth of

Oh, the depth of the

Oh, the depth of the riches … (and so on)

DAY 3

God's People in a Pagan World

When Daniel and his three young friends were taken to Babylon—the same land in which the story of Esther takes place more than a century later—they stood out from the pagans of that land and also from their fellow Jews, who had conformed to the Babylonian culture. Daniel and his friends are referred to in the Hebrew's "Faith Hall of Fame" as those who "shut the mouths of lions" and "quenched the fury of the flames" (Heb. 11:33–34).

Read Daniel 1:3–5.

7. What preparations did Daniel and the other young men undergo in order to serve the king? (vv. 4–5)

More than a century later, a parallel event took place under a different king.

Read Esther 2:2–4, 12.

8. Which young women were chosen to serve the king? How did they prepare?

Daniel and his friends Shadrach, Meshach, and Abednego faced enormous pressure to deny their faith and engage in the immoral practices planned by King Nebuchadnezzar. It's important to see this, for God's people in the book of Esther were faced with similar pressures and responded quite differently, at least initially.

What similarities, if any, do you see between this account and the account in Daniel?

Read Daniel 1:6–21.

9. What step of faith did Daniel and his friends take?

In what ways do you see God at work in their lives in this passage?

Read Daniel 3.

10. What did King Nebuchadnezzar command the people to do? (vv. 1–6)

11. What step of faith did Shadrach, Meshach, and Abednego take? (vv. 12–15) What did they say to the king? (vv. 16–18)

12. Briefly describe what happened to Daniel's friends when they refused to comply with the king's edict. (vv. 19–30)

What evidence do you see of God at work in this situation?

Read Esther 4—5. (This overview is optional but strongly recommended.)
Summarize each chapter in a sentence or two.

Detective for the Divine

In what ways have you seen God at work in your life in the past twenty-four hours?

DAY 4
. . . .

The Jews Are Allowed to Go Home

Just as Jeremiah prophesied, after seventy years of captivity, God punished the king of Babylon. (This occurred between 539 and 536 BC.) The Persians, led by Cyrus, besieged and conquered Babylon. Not long after this, Cyrus gave the Jews the freedom to choose whether to return to Jerusalem or stay in what was now part of the Persian Empire (see Ezra 1:1–4). Nearly fifty thousand Jews, many of them devout, were in the first group that returned to Jerusalem. A number of Bible commentators, such as J. Vernon McGee, believe that those who stayed were "out of the will of God."[7]

More than two hundred years before Esther, Isaiah prophesied that Cyrus, who hadn't even been born, would free the Jews. Note the phrase, "though you have not known Me" in the prophecy (Isa. 45:4 NASB). Then just fifty years or so before Esther, Isaiah's prophecy was finally fulfilled when Cyrus freed the Jews.

Providence. God cares. God has a plan. God is in control. And He can use anyone He chooses to accomplish His purposes.

Read Isaiah 44:21—45:13.

13. Summarize what you learn about the following in Isaiah's prophecy:

A. God's feelings for His people (44:21–22)

B. God (44:24–26; 45:5–7, 9–12)

C. Cyrus of Persia (44:28—45:4, 13)

14. God can use anyone, even those who don't acknowledge Him. What does Proverbs 21:1 say?

Read Ezra 1:1 and briefly discuss how Proverbs 21:1 was reflected in Cyrus's decision to free God's people.

15. What do you learn from the prophecies in Isaiah about God's involvement in the world He created?

Read Ezra 1—2.

16. Briefly describe the events in this passage that fulfill the prophecies of Jeremiah and Isaiah. (See Jeremiah 25:1–14 and Isaiah 44:28; 45:13 to refresh your memory.)

The tomb of Cyrus still exists in what is now Iran. Although the inscription is now illegible, it was preserved in the writings of the ancient Greek biographer Plutarch (AD 90):

> *O man, whosoever thou art and whencesoever thou comest, for I know that thou wilt come, I am Cyrus and I won for the Persians their empire. Do not, therefore, begrudge me this little earth which covers my body.*[8]

17. As you consider God's intricate plan and see it actually unfolding in Scripture, what impact does it have on you personally?

Read Esther 6—8. (This overview is optional but strongly recommended.)

Summarize each of these chapters in a sentence or two.

Memory Work

Spend a few minutes reviewing your memory verse.

DAY 5

Some Jews Choose to Stay in Persia

Many Bible commentators believe that the Jews who chose to stay in Persia rather than return to Jerusalem did so because they had become comfortable in this pagan land. By the time of Esther, God's people had become so assimilated into the Persian culture that they had lost their cultural and religious identity. You may notice, for example, that none of the Persians seemed to know that Mordecai was a Jew, even though he had lived in this land all of his life. It was only in the midst of crisis that his identity was revealed.

In *The Expositor's Bible Commentary*, F. B. Huey Jr. states that "the hiddenness of God can sometimes be explained as evidence of His displeasure" (Amos 8:11; Ezek. 11:23).[9] This may explain God's silence in the book of Esther. As author John Brug writes, "The secular tone of the book reflects the conditions and attitudes of Jews scattered in Persia rather than those of pious Jews in the Holy Land."[10]

Whatever the reason for God's silence in the book of Esther, His fingerprints are everywhere. He is the real Hero of the story.

It gives me great hope to see that God didn't forsake His people, even when their behavior grieved Him. As the prophet Jeremiah wrote, "Because of the LORD's great love, we are not consumed" (Lam. 3:22). I have often failed my Lord. I'm a chipped pot, and yet I long for Him to use me. Will He ever give up on me? Not as long as I keep coming back to Him. Not as long as I allow His gentle hands to mend me, mold me, and make me a vessel fit to be used.

Studying the book of Esther is challenging because there are so many differing views about Mordecai and Esther and the parts they played in this biblical drama. When the book of Esther is read in Jewish homes during Purim (the celebration of God's deliverance of the Jewish people through Esther), children boo when Haman's name is read, and they cheer loudly each time the names of Esther or Mordecai are mentioned. To these children, Esther and Mordecai are heroes because they intervened on behalf of the Jewish people and saved them from annihilation. Considering the enormous suffering God's people have experienced throughout history, it's understandable that Esther, who risked her life for her people, would be considered a heroine. And she is indeed a heroine. Yet even heroes and heroines have feet of clay.

A woman once said to me,

> When I heard you speak on the book of Esther and you asked us to consider whether or not Mordecai should have asked Esther to hide her faith and sleep with the king, I was shocked and offended. All during my childhood, Esther was presented to me as the perfect woman. So I had trouble listening to you with hearing ears. But in time I've come to realize that I'm wading into treacherous water when I expect any person to be perfect. People can be models for us, but only God can be our foundation.

As that wonderful old hymn "The Solid Rock" says, "I dare not trust the sweetest frame, but wholly lean on Jesus' name."[11]

Personally I prefer seeing Esther and Mordecai not as icons to be worshiped but as real people who walked in the fear of man until God brought them to their senses. I agree with F. B. Huey Jr., who wrote,

> Criticism of the morality of Esther and Mordecai is no more an attack on the inspiration of the Scriptures than a condemnation of the idolatry of the Israelites during the monarchy is an attack on the Scriptures.[12]

Understanding this impacts how we see not only the book of Esther but also all of Scripture. Before we assume that someone is a positive role model, we should examine his or her behavior in the light of Scripture, particularly those Scriptures that teach us how to live. For example, both David and Solomon had many wives. But can you think of any teaching in the Bible that supports polygamy? Can you think of any teaching that refutes it? (In Matthew 19:4–8, for instance, we see that God's plan is for one man and one woman to unite for life.) Therefore, even though David was a man after God's own heart, we shouldn't imitate his polygamous lifestyle.

Don't be afraid to hold the behavior of Esther or Mordecai up to the plumb line of Scripture. And don't be devastated when you discover that they don't always measure up. No person should ever be worshiped. God alone is worthy of our worship. Even if Esther and Mordecai were at times out of God's will, He still cared for them. What hope that gives me, His erring child!

17

Songs of Praise

During your personal quiet time today, sing (or read aloud) the hymn "The Solid Rock."

Read 1 Corinthians 10:1–13.

18. According to verses 6 and 11, why did God give us negative examples of people in Scripture?

19. How can Scripture help us determine if a biblical character's behavior is pleasing or displeasing to God?

Read Esther 9—10. (This overview is optional but strongly recommended.)

Summarize each of these chapters in a sentence or two.

Memory Work

Spend a few minutes reviewing your memory verse for the week.

Detective for the Divine

How have you seen God working in your life in the past twenty-four hours?

What do you think you'll remember about this week's lesson? What steps can you take to apply these things to your life?

Prayer Time

This week the discussion leader will close in prayer.

Two

"He Who Sits in the Heavens Laughs"

The second psalm paints a picture of God watching the rulers of the earth conspiring together against the Lord. The psalmist says, "He who sits in the heavens laughs" (Ps. 2:4 NASB). This is a laugh of scorn, of anger, and of amazement that humans are so consumed with themselves and so completely unaware of the God who made them.

Although the events in Esther's life took place long ago (more than twenty-five centuries ago) and far away (in the Persian Empire, which stretched from India to Greece and Egypt to Ethiopia), the values and the empty pursuits of people during that time sound just like the values and the empty pursuits of people today. Our world seems like a mirror of Esther's world, a world obsessed with wealth, power, entertainment, youth and beauty, sexual immorality, and alcohol.

Esther is one of the few books of the Bible in which the story takes place outside the Holy Land. It was difficult for God's people to live in the decadent culture of Persia and not be pulled down. How relevant for us today!

It isn't easy to live in this world and not be of it. It isn't easy to maintain an eternal perspective when those around us, even many believers, have an "under the sun" perspective (Eccl. 1:14), a perspective that focuses on the visible and loses sight of the invisible. It isn't easy for us as women to resist believing the lie that our real worth is in our physical appearance and allure when the media continually bombards us with this message. Even within the Christian community, there are pressures that can make women think that their gifts are limited to the church nursery and the kitchen. But God has a much greater plan.

The secret to being steadfast in a world of strong tides is to be anchored to the Lord and His Word. It's imperative for us who live in a contemporary Persia to cling to that anchor with all of our hearts, with all of our souls, and with all of our minds. It's imperative that we relinquish our false gods, that we stop running to the television, binging on food, or seeking praise from people to give us our sense of well-being, and that we run instead to the Lover of our souls—to our Lord Jesus.

Prepare Your Heart to Hear

Before you begin each of the following daily lessons, determine to listen to the Lord. The world shouts, but God whispers. So be still and listen for His voice.

Memory Work

Over the next eight weeks, you'll work on committing Esther 4:12–16 to memory:

> *When Esther's words were reported to Mordecai, he sent back this answer: "Do not think that because you are in the king's house you alone of all the Jews will escape. For if you remain silent at this time, relief and deliverance for the Jews will arise from another place, but you and your father's family will perish. And who knows but that you have come to this royal position for such a time as this?"*

> *Then Esther sent this reply to Mordecai: "Go, gather together all the Jews who are in Susa, and fast for me. Do not eat or drink for three days, night or day. I and my maids will fast as you do. When this is done, I will go to the king, even though it is against the law. And if I perish, I perish."*

Memorizing such a long passage may seem daunting, but it will be well worth the effort. Even though you may not see it at first, this passage is filled with golden nuggets that will transform your life. If you hide it in your heart, it will help to keep you soaring above the decadence of this world long after you've finished this study. This week focus only on memorizing verses 12 and 13. Remember that memorizing a word at a time will help seal the passage in your mind.

> *When Esther's words were reported to Mordecai, he sent back this answer: "Do not think that because you are in the king's house you alone of all the Jews will escape."*

WARMUP

When I was young, my dreams were for the cotton-candy stuff of being beautiful, rich, or popular. And though those desires still flit into my head, my dreams have truly changed as I've discovered the excitement of knowing God, as I've buried my fifty-nine-year-old beloved husband, as I've seen the dreams of my youth melt. I desire the things that can never fade; I pray to see each of my children and grandchildren have a vibrant love relationship with Jesus; I long to be quickened by the Spirit of God in my writing and speaking; and I dream of being like Jesus.

Share a transitory dream you have (e.g., a new home, a healthier body, a new job, the recognition of others); then share an eternal dream (e.g., the salvation of a loved one, using the gifts God has given you to minister to others, showing Jesus' love to a hurting world). Be concise. (Give women the freedom to pass.)

DAY I
• •

The Worldly Perspective of the Book of Esther

The party that opens the book of Esther, though it occurred more than twenty-five centuries ago, sounds strikingly like a celebrity wedding. Consider some of the ways *People* magazine described Donald Trump's wedding to Slovenian model Melania Knauss:

> The billionaire lord of real estate and reality TV and his Slovenian bride began life together—with the help of 45 chefs, 28 seamstresses, 100 limousine drivers and the guys who drove dozens of refrigerated trucks with some 10,000 flowers from New York to Florida to provide the all-white roses, hydrangeas, gardenias and peonies the bride had her heart set on ...

> Knauss's Christian Dior gown was made for her in Paris by 28 seamstresses, who spent more than 1,000 hours on the project—550 doing the embroidery and sewing on 1,500 rhinestones ...

> Pastry chef Cedric Barbaret spent two months creating nearly 3,000 roses from icing for the 5-ft. orange Grand Marnier chiffon cake, which weighed 200 lbs. "It took five guys to carry it," he says.... The guests were served $650 bottles of champagne.[1]

Now consider the six-month-long party—a perpetual smorgasbord of gold, glitz, and glamour—that Xerxes threw to impress the military leaders, princes, and nobles of his empire.

Read Esther 1.

1. Listing words and phrases from the text, describe the wealth and power King Xerxes displayed. According to verses 10 and 11, what else did the king want to put on display? Why?

2. What similarities do you see between this event and Donald Trump's wedding?

3. There is an enormous satire throughout Esther, and you are getting a taste of it in this opening chapter. What hyperbole do you see? What phrases indicate that Xerxes might have thought himself to be like a god?

4. The world in which Esther lived was obsessed with visible, temporary things. What do the following passages say about this?

   A. Romans 12:2

      B. 2 Corinthians 4:18

      C. Colossians 3:1–10

Read Ecclesiastes 2:1–11.

    5. Solomon believed in God, yet he lost his eternal perspective. Caught up in the mind-set of the world—the "under the sun" perspective—he chased after transitory things. Briefly describe Solomon's pursuits and how they affected him.

Read the following famous quote from C. S. Lewis.

> We are half-hearted creatures, fooling about with drink and sex and ambition when infinite joy is offered to us, like an ignorant child who wants to go on making mud pies in a slum because he cannot imagine what is meant by the offer of a holiday at the sea.[2]

    6. How does the above thought apply to the lives of the people we've been reading about? Have you found this to be true in your own life? Explain.

    7. As you examine your own heart and life, can you honestly say that Jesus is your first love? When you wake up in the morning, are your thoughts drawn to Him? Are you eager to run to Him, to feast on His Word? What do you think about? What do you talk about?

Detective for the Divine

How have you sensed God at work in your life in the past twenty-four hours through His Word, His presence, and His provision?

DAY 2

Satire, Women, and Eunuchs

In the early seventies a TV show called *All in the Family* was very popular. Archie Bunker, the lead character, portrayed a bigot. He demeaned everyone who wasn't like him: minority groups, women (including his own wife and daughter), and his son-in-law whom he called "Meathead." Some who watched the sitcom didn't see the satire or the foolishness and danger of Archie's depraved attitudes; instead, they applauded him. Watching the show only reinforced their godless attitudes of prejudice and hate. They should have laughed *at* Archie, not *with* him.

Likewise, it's vital that we see the satire in the book of Esther. Even though there's no editorial commentary, so much of what is written is tongue in cheek. God may be silent in this story, but He uses satire to help us see the foolishness of those who live their lives apart from Him as well as their distorted thinking, their prideful plans, and the ostentatious way in which they carry them out.

As we read earlier in Psalm 2, "He who sits in the heavens laughs" (v. 4 NASB) at the world's rulers, who are obsessed with themselves and "take counsel together, against … his anointed" (v. 2 KJV). This isn't a laugh of delight, but of scorn, a holy wrath at those who think they can oppose God and His ways.

Songs of Praise

Sing "In My Life, Lord" during your personal quiet time.

In some Bible versions Xerxes is called "King Ahasuerus," which is really a reference to his Persian title rather than his name. His Greek name was Xerxes, and the Greek historian Herodotus described him as "impatient, hot-tempered, and lecherous."[3] He was the grandson of Cyrus the Great (the Persian king who freed the Jews more than fifty years earlier) and the son of Darius. Darius had suffered a humiliating defeat by the Greeks, and his son continued the effort to expand the Persian Empire to include Greece. The six-month party with which the book of Esther opens was probably a military planning session. Xerxes clearly wanted to succeed where his father had failed and become king of the whole world—or so he thought. (The only land he knew of over which he didn't already reign was Greece.) But he wouldn't be able to conquer Greece without the wholehearted support of all the military leaders in his provinces. So he put on an extravagant display of his wealth.

Joyce Baldwin comments on the difference between the opulent Persian palace of Xerxes and the lean life of most of his subjects. Then, as now, most people in western Asia had hard lives, and food was none too plentiful. The palace at Susa was elevated 120 feet to emphasize the supremacy of the king.[4]

At the end of this six-month extravaganza, Xerxes threw a seven-day drinking party. (This was a stag party for all the men in the city. The queen was having her own party with the women in another part of the palace.) On the final day of the bash, the king, whose judgment was impaired by wine, decided to liven things up by parading his lovely wife, Vashti, before these men who had been drinking for days without restraint.

The ancient historian Josephus wrote that Vashti was to appear before the guests in the nude, wearing only her royal crown.[5] Whether or not Josephus is correct, it's clear that the king's demand was demeaning, like asking Vashti to pop out of a cardboard cake.

But Vashti refused to come. *Surprise!* All that hype and effort down the drain. Instead of the party ending with a bang, it ends in humiliation for the enraged king. The lights don't go on. The curtain doesn't go up. The queen will not obey her husband.

Review Esther 1:1–12.

8. According to verses 3 and 4, what was the purpose of the king's first party?

Describe the atmosphere of the second party (including furnishings, decorations, and hospitality. See vv. 5–8).

9. Using a dictionary, define the following words:

A. eunuch

B. castrate

10. In verse 10, we learn that the king had seven eunuchs who served him. What does this tell you about Persian culture at the time and the attitude toward people?

11. Why do you think Xerxes ordered seven eunuchs to escort one woman?

Perhaps the king wanted his eunuchs to carry Vashti into the party on some sort of a platform. In *The Pulpit Commentary,* W. Dinwiddie writes,

> The emphatic way in which the number and names of the chamberlains are given seems to indicate that there was some fear of the queen in the king's heart. He knew her character, and was not unconscious of the insult implied in his command.... He perhaps hoped by this parade to overcome any objection she might have to obey his strange command. But the quality of evil is not affected by the garnishings with which men clothe and try to conceal it.[6]

Review Esther 1:13–21.

12. The following verses illustrate some of the continuing satire in the latter half of Esther 1. See if you can discover why God may be "laughing" in each passage.

    A. verses 13–15

    B. verses 16–18

    C. verses 19–20

    D. verses 20–21

13. Based on your observations of Esther 1, what do you think the attitude toward women was in this culture? (List some verses to support your answer.)

14. What does this passage tell you about Xerxes and his perspective on life? (Include what was important to him, the value he placed on people, and anything else you can discern from the text.)

Xerxes mistreated the poor, the helpless, and women. He was obsessed with wine, wealth, and entertainment. All that mattered to him was his own selfish agenda and status. Believers can also be swept up in the tides of the times if they aren't clinging to God and His Word.

15. Answer the following questions, asking God to help you be honest with yourself and Him:

    A. Do I show favoritism to the beautiful, rich, or powerful?

    B. Do I understand that I, as a woman, can be used mightily for His glory, as Esther was? Or have I limited my view of myself, holding myself back, seeing myself through man's eyes instead of God's?

Memory Work

Spend a few minutes reviewing your memory verses.

DAY 3

An Angry King

Xerxes is well known in secular history for his temper. Many feel he suffered from some sort of mental abnormality (as has been true of many leaders, such as Nebuchadnezzar, Napoléon, Hitler, and Saddam Hussein) that revealed itself in hysterical fits of rage. Historians report that Xerxes once sailed a fleet of three hundred ships to Salamis in an attempt to conquer Greece. (This probably occurred after his six-month-long party.) But the entire fleet was destroyed by the waves, and Xerxes had the sea whipped for the offense!

The historian Herodotus recorded an incident that shows the enormous callousness of Xerxes. Pythius of Lydia, rumored to be the second-richest man on earth, offered to finance Xerxes' war with Greece, but in return he requested a small favor. With five of his sons already pledged to serve in the war, he asked if the eldest could remain at home to care for his aging father. In a rage Xerxes ordered that this son be cut in half. The two halves of the body were then placed on either side of the road, and the army marched between them. After carrying out this vicious act, Xerxes said to Pythius, "There, now you can keep your son at home!"

In *When God Weeps,* Joni Eareckson Tada and Steven Estes comment on this incident, contrasting Xerxes, who had no compassion for his subjects, and God, who was willing to be "cut in half," so to speak, to die on a cross so that we might live.[7]

Research shows that one of the strongest male drives is for status. God can use this drive to help men accomplish good things. But if a man doesn't find his identity in Christ, status can easily become the god of his life. This seems to have been true of Xerxes, who had an overwhelming drive for status, judging by the descriptions of his opulent palace in Esther 1:4–7. Archaeologists confirmed this when they uncovered Xerxes' palace at Susa.[8] Inscriptions have also been found in which Xerxes referred to himself as "the great King, the King of Kings, the King of the lands occupied by many races, the King of this great world."[9] Is this a man you would dare to embarrass publicly?

Review Esther 1:12–22.

16. After his humiliation, whom did Xerxes consult? What do you learn about these men in verses 13 and 14?

    Considering Xerxes' temperament, what kind of counsel would you expect his advisers to give him? Explain.

17. Summarize Memucan's counsel and reasoning (vv. 16–20). In light of the Persian culture and the attitude toward women, do you think this was a valid concern or an overreaction? Explain.

18. What do you learn about the laws of the Medes and Persians in verse 19?

19. What subtle change do you see in the way Memucan refers to the queen in verse 19? Do you think this omission had any special significance? Explain.

20. Describe the backlash Vashti experienced as a result of her refusal to obey the king. (vv. 16–22)

21. How effective do you think Memucan's law was in ensuring that women respected their husbands? How might you have responded to such a law?

22. According to radio pastor Woodrow Kroll, "The key to respect is not a demand; it is a demonstration. It's love, it's honor, it's looking out for the needs of your wife, it's helping your wife to grow in faith."[10] Do you agree? Explain.

What causes you to respect a man?

Personal Action Assignment

Think of a man in your life whom you respect and could encourage. Write him a note or e-mail telling him the things you see in his life that cause you to respect him. If you feel comfortable doing so, share what you wrote with the group.

Detective for the Divine

In what ways has your love or understanding of God grown in the past twenty-four hours?

DAY 4

Vashti, the Queen Who Said No

Did Vashti refuse to come to the party because she wanted to humiliate Xerxes? Did she refuse because she was a modest and virtuous woman who wouldn't compromise her standards and come before this drunken stag party? And how did she say no? Gently? We don't know.

What we can try to understand, with the help of didactic (teaching) scriptures, is what God asks of Christian wives. During the rest of this week, we'll be considering whether wives should obey their husbands in all circumstances. Views can vary widely among those who deeply love the Lord, so anticipate some good discussions in your group. Let's pray to discern the mind of God as we look closely at what Scripture has to say.

The first thing Scripture makes very clear is that wives are called to submit to their husbands. Yet to determine what this means, it's important that we define submission the way Scripture does and understand the difference between obedience and submission. Before you begin exploring this controversial subject, ask God to lead you into His truth, to give you an unbiased heart and mind, and to speak to you through His Word. (If you're single, this will still be relevant, not only because you may not always be single, but also because married friends might need your wise counsel.)

23. What do the following Scriptures teach us concerning marriage? Look at the context and discover all you can.

   A. Genesis 2:20–24

   B. Matthew 19:4–6

   C. 1 Corinthians 6:16

   D. Ephesians 5:31

24. What prevailing concept do you see in these passages?

   Note anything else you learned.

25. In a mysterious way, a marriage in which there is Christian unity reflects the love of God to the world. If you're married, how would those watching your relationship perceive the love of God?

Intriguingly, the word *obey* is used in Scripture concerning the relationship of children to their parents and children of God to their Heavenly Father, but it isn't used to describe the relationship of a wife to her husband. Instead, the word that is used in the Greek is translated "submit" in English. There is one New Testament incidence where the word *obey* is used in reference to a wife, but it is descriptive rather than prescriptive, describing the respectful attitude Sarah had toward Abraham (1 Pet. 3:6). Clearly, the marriage of Abraham and Sarah was not one of master and slave, for in one instance God told Abraham to do whatever Sarah told him to do (Gen. 21:12). Children (and children of God) are commanded to obey, but wives are not.

Yet in the pagan setting of the book of Esther, the king became enraged and reacted impulsively because Vashti refused to obey him. The satire here is thick, so we must consider what God is actually saying. When Christ came, He elevated wives from a slave-master or child-parent relationship to a position as coheirs with their husbands. (See 1 Peter 3:7.) God never intended husbands to dominate their wives in order to use them and take advantage of them. Instead, He called husbands to sacrifice themselves for their wives and continually lift them up. And He called wives to submit to their husbands, continually lifting them up so that together they are mutually built up and glorify God with their love and harmony. This is far different from the picture of domination we see in Esther.

So we see that submission normally occurs between equals, whereas obedience implies inequality, as with parent and child, master and slave, and even boss and employee. According to *Strong's Exhaustive Concordance,* the Greek term for submission, *hypotassō,* means "a voluntary attitude of giving in, cooperating." This word is used not only for wives with their husbands but also for the whole body of believers, so that we might live in harmony. It's an attitude of humble cooperation so that we might be unified in Christ and thereby bring glory to God. A woman is called to be an *ēzer,* "a help" in Hebrew—but this doesn't mean she's inferior, for the same word is used of God, who comes alongside and gives us His wisdom, His strength, and His love. A woman is a mighty warrior who helps her husband overcome spiritual enemies in this battle of life. Rather than "obeying" him when he asks her to sin, she gently speaks up (as we will see Esther do with her husband) so that she can truly help him be victorious over sin.

Submission is a foreign concept in a world where people want their own way and don't see the importance of living in harmony to bring glory to God. Submission calls for unselfishness, whether you're submitting to your husband, to another believer, or to God. It's a concept that should characterize the behavior of mature believers, whether male or female. Submission of all believers to one another is a thread that runs through the first letter of Peter and is intertwined with the thread of living holy lives, doing what is right, and trusting that God will honor us when we do.

26. Describe the context of submission in each of the following passages. Note anything else you learn.

   A. 1 Peter 2:13–15

   B. 1 Peter 2:18–20

C. 1 Peter 2:21–23 (note why Jesus was able to submit, for this is how we can find the power to submit as well)

D. 1 Peter 3:1

E. 1 Peter 3:7

F. 1 Peter 3:8

27. What common reason for submission do you see in these verses?

28. What is the general command to all believers in Ephesians 5:21?

What specific subcommands follow for each of these people?
A. wives (Eph. 5:22)

B. husbands (Eph. 5:25)

C. children (Eph. 6:1)

29. If you're married, do you have a spirit of humble cooperation with your husband? Do you refuse to manipulate? Do you consider his needs as well as your own? If not, why do you think you don't?

If you're single, do you have a spirit of cooperation with other believers? When you give up your own way, are you bitter or manipulative? If so, why does this grieve God?

Memory Work

Review your memory verses for this week.

DAY 5
● ●

When, If Ever, Should a Wife Defy Her Husband?

I once attended an event in which a respected woman author answered questions from the audience after finishing her presentation. One young woman stood and asked, "What advice would you give to the woman who is being abused by her husband?"

The author replied, "I would tell her to get down on her knees and ask God what she's doing to make her husband abuse her."

Several women walked out, and I empathized. Even though many men (and women) are in the grip of addiction, mental illness, or generational sin, no one has the right to be abusive. To assume that their abusive behavior is the fault of the victim is to exacerbate the sin. If we don't set boundaries when we're being abused, we only encourage the abuse. This isn't healthy for either partner.

Was Vashti right to refuse to obey her husband's immoral demand? Charles Swindoll writes,

> I applaud Queen Vashti for her courageous decision. Marriage does not give a husband the right or the license to fulfill his basest fantasies by using his wife as a sexual object.[11]

Sometimes a lack of obedience to an immoral demand may temporarily embarrass or punish a husband, but doing what is right is always in his best interest from an eternal point of view. Even though we don't know Vashti's motives in this situation, I agree that she should not have obeyed this immoral demand.

What does Scripture have to say about a wife's obeying the immoral demands of her husband? Should she set boundaries? Is it permissible for her to separate from (not divorce) her husband and insist that he get help for his abusive or immoral behavior? Let's consider this.

30. Some say that if a wife obeys an immoral demand from her husband, her husband, not she, will be held accountable. What does Romans 14:12 say?

31. In the book of Acts, the religious authorities ordered Peter and the other apostles to stop preaching about Christ (see Acts 4:1–21; 5:27–29). How did the apostles respond in Acts 4:19–20 and 5:29?

First Samuel 25 tells the story of a woman named Abigail, who, like Vashti, was married to a man who drank too much, had a temper, and made impetuous decisions. But God wasn't silent in this book as He was in Esther. He was clearly at work in the situation and used Abigail to avert disaster in spite of her husband's foolish behavior.

Read 1 Samuel 25:1–38.

32. Briefly summarize each of the following passages, noting any editorial commentary you find.

   A. verses 2–3

   B. verses 4–13

   C. verses 14–31

   D. verses 32–35

   E. verses 36–38

God sets boundaries to keep us from immoral and abusive behavior, and so must we. We must not condone and encourage sin in others. Dr. Henry Cloud and Dr. John Townsend write in their book *Boundaries,*

> We have never seen a "submission problem" that did not have a controlling husband at its root. When the wife begins to set clear boundaries, the lack of Christlikeness in a controlling husband becomes evident because the wife is no longer enabling his immature behavior. She is confronting the truth and setting biblical limits on hurtful behavior. Often, when the wife sets boundaries, the husband begins to grow up.[12]

33. When, if ever, do you think a wife is free to refuse a request or demand from her husband? Explain your reasoning. If you think she is free to refuse, how should she refuse?

34. Sometimes a woman will give in to her husband's immoral demands because she fears the consequences. For example, she may agree to lie to her husband's boss and say that her husband is sick when he's really drunk. According to 1 Peter 3:10–14, how should a woman in this situation respond to her husband?

35. How might a woman gently say no to her husband's request to watch pornographic movies or to cheat on the family's income tax, yet still express a spirit of submission?

Those who say that the fabric of Christianity will be torn apart if wives refuse to obey their husbands' immoral demands remind me of the scene in Esther 1 in which the king was enraged and hysterical about Vashti's refusal to obey him. This reaction, I believe, is largely unjustified. Yet I also believe that not submitting is a serious matter and shouldn't be done capriciously. As 1 Peter 3:4–5 tells us, God is pleased with a gentle and quiet spirit, with a woman who is supportive of her husband. God never calls us to support sin, but we must be careful to look at our motives. Before saying no, we need to make sure that we are truly taking a stand against sin rather than simply wanting our own way.

Memory Work

Spend several minutes reviewing your memory verses from this week as well as the first week.

Detective for the Divine

How have you sensed God at work in your life in the past twenty-four hours through His Word, His presence, and His provision?

Prayer Time

Many people are intimidated by the idea of praying aloud, so I've designed this exercise to lead you gently and gradually into group prayer. No one in this study will ever be forced to pray aloud.

One of the reasons that the fellowship of women is often warm and encouraging is that God has equipped most of us to be affirming. Giving a blessing to another woman through prayer is a wonderful gift. Today, stand in a circle holding hands and then, moving clockwise around the circle, have each woman bless the woman on her right in prayer.

For example, you might say something like this: "Thank You, Lord, for Linda and her warm smile." If you don't know Linda, you might say, "Lord, bless Linda." Or if you don't feel comfortable praying aloud, you can bless Linda silently and then squeeze the hand of the woman on your left, so that she will know it's her turn to give a blessing.

Three

The Contest for the New Miss Persia

The contest for the new Miss Persia involved twelve months of beauty treatments for every virgin in the king's harem, leading up to a night where each girl lost her virginity to the king. If Xerxes wasn't delighted with her and didn't summon her after that night, she would never again appear before him. But instead of returning to her family or the other virgins, she joined the king's concubines. (See Est. 2:12–14.)

A concubine gave the king the privileges of marriage, but she didn't receive honor in return. Instead, she was part of his harem. The women who were "taken" to the palace never saw their families again. These women's lives, though less horrific than the lives of girls today who are forced into the sex trade, were still destroyed. Concubines were robbed of their families, robbed of marriage, and robbed of honor. The whole sordid practice revealed the shallowness of the king and his advisers. Frederic Bush writes,

> The only measure of the woman who is fit to rule as queen by the king's side is her beauty of figure and face and her performance in his bed![1]

It distresses me when commentators tiptoe around this chapter or make light of it instead of soundly condemning the great sin that was committed against these young women and the families who loved them. I'm thankful to those who do condemn it. W. Clarkson, for example, offers this commentary on Esther 2:

> One of the very worst consequences of the reign of sin in this world is the degradation of woman. Meant to be man's helpmeet and companion as he walks the path of life, she became, under its dominion, the mere victim of his ignoble passion.[2]

When I think about the hundreds, perhaps thousands, of young women who were forcibly taken from their families to become sex objects and slaves, I'm filled with grief. (The trafficking of women and children has gone on for thousands of years, and even today many young girls are being sold into a life of horror.)[3]

We don't know how old Esther was when she was taken. She was old enough to be sexually appealing, but I suspect she was young, for she was unmarried, and women then were usually married by their middle teens. She had always obeyed Mordecai, as a good daughter would, so I tend to put the greater weight of responsibility on him. However, it is also true that Esther was old enough to have taken a stand, and I certainly cannot agree with the commentators who applaud Mordecai and Esther or who say they "didn't have a choice." We always have a choice, even though that choice may be death. Esther's ancestors (Daniel and his friends) were willing to die rather than to compromise their obedience to God. In *Lost Women of the Bible*, Carolyn Custis James writes,

> The first time I began to see Esther's flaws, I felt like I was losing something precious. Here was one of the rare legendary women of the Bible …then someone had to go spoil it all by pointing out her faults….
>
> Over time, I've come to see the value of being as honest about people in the Bible as the Bible is…. We'll never find ourselves in Esther's story if we convince ourselves she's perfect…. Esther lost her way when she accepted the culture's view that beauty was all she had to offer. She forgot she was Hadassah—a daughter of the covenant, a descendant of Abraham and Sarah, and God's image bearer…. Her purpose slipped from pleasing God to making Xerxes happy…. According to God's blueprint for women, Esther was seriously off mission.[4]

Of course, it's easy to be critical of Esther. After all, we aren't the ones faced with the prospect of taking a stand before a capricious king, of saying, "Before God I cannot sleep with you." But in seeing Esther's failure, we can also more clearly see her courageous U-turn when she finally does go to the king to take a stand for right, knowing full well that she may perish. May we be inspired to make the U-turns we need to make to get back on mission with God whenever we realize that we've wandered from that mission.

Prepare Your Heart to Hear

Sing (or read) "Open Our Eyes, Lord" each day before you begin the lesson.

Memory Work

Continue memorizing Esther 4:12–13 until you can repeat it accurately.

> *When Esther's words were reported to Mordecai, he sent back this answer: "Do not think that because you are in the king's house you alone of all the Jews will escape."*

WARMUP

Imagine being one of the contestants going through twelve months of beauty treatments in the king's palace (Est. 2:12). What do you think you might have felt (e.g, homesickness, rivalry, fear, helplessness)? What impact do you think this atmosphere might have had on your identity as a woman?

DAY 1

The Search for Beautiful Young Virgins

An extensive search was made for beautiful young virgins who would enter the king's harem and possibly become the next queen. Commissioners were appointed to find them in every one of the 127 provinces over which Xerxes reigned—an area bigger than the United States. Joyce Baldwin speaks of the horror that must have been caused by the roundup of these girls.[5] As the mother of three daughters, I would be devastated if any of my daughters were taken for this purpose, knowing I would never see them again and that they, most likely, would become concubines. In the movie *Memoirs of a Geisha*, there are many parallels to the events in Esther, though the setting is different. The movie begins in horror as two defenseless little girls are suddenly wrenched from their home and locked in an oxcart. They cry out in terror, pressing against the bars, pleading with their father as he stands there watching. Having just lost his wife, he feels forced into selling his daughters. He watches as they disappear from sight, tears rolling down his cheeks. Their fate is the sex trade. One will become a prostitute and the other will enter the world of the geishas, but both are destined for a loveless life. Although the sister who was chosen to be a geisha was told that it was an honor, she soon learns the truth.[6] Like the contestants in Xerxes' contest, a geisha is robbed of what every woman holds dear: true love.

How many girls were wrenched from their homes for Xerxes' immoral contest? The ancient historian Josephus estimated that 400 were taken.[7] Historian Paton speculates that one virgin taken each night for four years (see Est. 1:3; 2:16) would have totaled 1,460.[8] However, the contest may not have lasted four years, for historians believe that during much of the time between the third and seventh years of Xerxes' reign, he was away battling Greece. The historian Herodotus wrote that Xerxes came home defeated and consoled himself with his harem. The word "later" with which the second chapter of Esther begins may refer to the war with Greece.

Read Esther 2.

1. Write down your observations of this chapter.

   Based on your observations, what seems praiseworthy? What seems to fall short of God's standard? (Record specific verses.)

2. What do we learn about King Xerxes in verse 1?

   If Vashti was still around and Xerxes could have reinstated her, why might that have been a problem for the king's counselors?

3. What did the counselors propose to Xerxes? (v. 4) How did he respond?

What is your impression of Xerxes' counselors? Explain.

4. Summarize the following passages and explain how they show the honor God places on virginity.

A. Genesis 24:15–16

B. Deuteronomy 22:13–21

C. Song of Songs 4:12

5. A virgin bride is precious in God's sight because she symbolizes the purity He longs for in us. What does 2 Corinthians 11:2 say about this?

6. Whether we're single or married, Scripture is clear that we're to remain sexually pure. What are some ways we can hold to this standard personally and help the next generation hold to it?

Detective for the Divine

How have you experienced God's presence in your life in the past twenty-four hours? (See Ps. 34:15.)

DAY 2

Squeezed into the World's Mold

Did Mordecai encourage Esther to take part in this contest? Some commentators think he was politically ambitious and arranged for Esther to be taken into the king's harem because he thought she would win. It's possible, but I believe the evidence is strong that Mordecai cared deeply for Esther. In fact, after reading about all the abuse toward women in this culture, it's a relief to finally come to a verse that shows tenderness: "Mordecai had taken [Esther] as his own daughter when her father and mother died" (Est. 2:7).

Mordecai, who was Esther's much older cousin, had taken her in and become like a father to her. The love between them is evident throughout the book. I doubt therefore that he arranged for her to participate in such a sordid contest. *The Expositor's Bible Commentary* agrees, saying that fathers "apparently did not voluntarily present their daughters as evidenced by the king's appointment of officials to search for the candidates."[9] Likewise, a "tight series of three passive verbs [Est. 2:8] ... was proclaimed ... were gathered ... was taken, portray an irresistible series of events."[10]

However, even if Mordecai didn't volunteer Esther for this contest, he did tell her to hide her faith. How long did she keep silent? Five, possibly seven years (compare Esther 2:16 with Esther 3:7). What did that involve? Certainly eating the king's unkosher food (as Daniel refused to do) and perhaps idol worship (as Shadrach, Meshach, and Abednego refused to do). She couldn't explain that her religion told her not to sleep with a man to whom she wasn't married. Why did Mordecai tell her to hide her faith? He couldn't have anticipated the future edict to annihilate the Jewish people, but he may have feared anti-Semitism. Even though he was a Jew, he clearly wasn't living in such a way that his faith was obvious to his non-Jewish neighbors in Susa. Carl Armerding writes, "The fact that he had to tell others that he [was] a Jew is interesting (Esther 3:4). He had lived so long in Persia that he must have become like them."[11]

Mordecai falls short when we compare him to Daniel here, but I think he was genuinely grieved when the king's commissioners came for Esther. He paced back and forth outside the palace harem, continually trying to find out how his daughter was and what was happening to her (2:11). He was obviously frantic. Surely he knew that it was wrong for Esther to commit a sexually immoral act and marry a Gentile, but he also must have feared for her taking a stand, feared, quite legitimately, for her life. J. Vernon McGee has attributed Mordecai's anxiety, however, to being out of the will of God. Instead of having the peace of knowing that he was under the shadow of God's wings, he was "nervously biting [his] fingernails, wondering how it [would] all turn out."[12]

I tend to see Mordecai as the one who should be held primarily accountable, but that may not be fair. It's important for us as women to realize we can't blame the men in our lives for our own choices, even when the pressure is great. Esther was young, but she wasn't a child. Carolyn Custis James believes that Esther got lost in her culture, and it's easy for us to do the same:

> Esther's claim to fame was her beauty and her ability to please.... If she were alive today she'd be featured on the covers of fashion magazines and hounded by the paparazzi whenever she stepped out.... The ancient culture in which she lived, like a lot of times and places in the world, (most of them, to be honest) was a place where men noticed and valued a woman for her looks and her readiness to submit. In such a social climate, it was only a matter of time before Esther got discovered. She got lost in beauty treatments, perfumed oils, and in her studied, skillful efforts to comply with the men in her life.[13]

Review Esther 2:5–11.

7. What do you learn about Mordecai in verses 5 and 6?

The phrasing "who had been carried into exile" (v. 6) is confusing, but it probably refers to Kish rather than Mordecai, for the exile had begun more than a century earlier. The phrasing reflects the strong family solidarity among the Jews; in a sense, Mordecai and Kish were one.

8. Read Daniel 1 and 3 and summarize the differences you see between the behavior of Mordecai's ancestors in a pagan land and Mordecai's behavior in a pagan land.

9. Do you think Mordecai volunteered Esther for the contest? Why or why not?

10. As mothers (or mentors, if you don't have children), we can encourage our children to be comfortable and safe (but out of the will of God) or to live wholeheartedly for Christ, no matter the cost. In what kinds of situations might we be faced with this choice?

11. List some of the disadvantages of being incredibly beautiful.

Memory Work

Spend a few minutes reviewing your memory verses.

DAY 3

God Gave Esther Favor

There is great consolation in this story for any woman who has been the victim of sexual abuse. Esther was taken from her home, told to comply with the king's wishes, and did what most young teens would have done. She didn't have friends to stand with her (as Shadrach, Meshach, and Abednego did), nor did she have a godly mentor as these young men had in Daniel. Some fictionalized accounts of Esther try to turn Xerxes into a romantic and kind king, but this isn't supported by history or by the Scriptures. The fact is that this young girl lost her virginity to a lecherous and cruel king.

I don't know why God allows sexual abuse, but I do know that He hasn't lost control. He sees, He cares, and He will bring beauty out of ashes.

This seems to be reflected in Esther's name Hadassah, which means "myrtle." As Joyce Baldwin writes,

The myrtle would replace the briars and thorns of the desert, so depicting the Lord's forgiveness and acceptance of his people. Myrtle branches are still carried in procession at the Feast of the Tabernacles and signify peace and thanksgiving. The Persian equivalent, Esther, "star" (cf. Steila), picks up the sound of the Hebrew and suggests the star-like flowers of the myrtle.[14]

Esther impressed the eunuch in charge of the virgins. Usually the eunuch in this role was "a repulsive old man"[15] who had political influence. But Esther "pleased him and won his favor" (Est. 2:9). The Hebrew word for "favor" is the covenant word *hesed* and is used again in verse 17. It's an intriguing word in a secular setting and seems to imply that God's hand was upon her. (This is the same word used in Daniel 1:9 when we're told that God gave Daniel favor in the eyes of his Babylonian overseer.) Another similarity some see between Esther and Daniel is restraint. Just as Daniel refused the king's rich food, Esther refused to ask the king for more than the king's eunuch suggested, which presumably meant that she refused to ask for the extravagant clothing and jewelry that the other young women wore (Est. 2:15).

Songs of Praise

During your quiet time, sing (or read aloud) "Seek Ye First" and "As the Deer." (You can find these praise songs in many hymnals and on the Internet.)

Review Esther 2:7–10.

12. Write down everything you discover about Esther in these verses.

13. What do the following passages say about the myrtle? What relationship do you see between these passages and Hadassah, whose name means "myrtle"?

    A. Isaiah 41:19

    B. Isaiah 55:13

14. What impact did Esther have on Hegai, the eunuch in charge of the king's virgins? (v. 9)

15. What do you learn about hesed—favor, loyal love, faithfulness, and kindness—from the following passages?

    A. Proverbs 19:22

    B. Proverbs 20:6

C. Proverbs 31:26

16. When you think of a woman who wins hesed or favor with others, what images come to mind?

17. Are you a woman who has received and displays hesed? Explain. Write down anything the Lord may be impressing on your heart right now.

Detective for the Divine

In what ways have you experienced God's provision in the past twenty-four hours? (See Matt. 6:33.)

DAY 4

The Contest

As we've been reading, Esther, along with the other virgins, had twelve months of beauty treatments. For six months she was bathed and rubbed with oils so that her skin would be soft, touchable, and sweet smelling for the king. Myrrh was also used for its purifying powers. Then during the final six months, various cosmetics were applied until the desired effect was achieved.

Joyce Baldwin describes some of the practices used in Iran and north India during ancient times, and even today, to prepare a woman for her wedding day: "There is ritual cleansing at the communal bathhouse, the plucking of eyebrows and removal of body hair, the painting of hands and feet with henna, and a paste applied to lighten the skin and to remove spots and blemishes."[16] Carl Armerding points out, "Nothing is said about any intellectual or spiritual preparation."[17] Armerding also suspects that the long period for purification must have occurred because the king was considered almost divine, and had double standards, demanding utmost purity from the girl but with no thought of offering her the same.

We're told that after these beauty treatments, each virgin spent a night with Xerxes. After this, she went to live with the king's concubines. Only one virgin would win the contest and become queen. The others would likely never see the king again unless he was pleased with one of them and called for her by name (Est. 2:14). I wonder what would have happened if instead of complying, Esther had approached the king humbly and said in the manner of her godly ancestors, "I mean you no disrespect, O king, but I worship the one true God, and before Him, I cannot do what you ask. I believe my God can deliver me, but even if He does not, I cannot do this."

We will never know because Esther didn't take a stand.

I have sympathy for Esther; Mordecai, whom she trusted and had always obeyed, told her to hide her faith and comply. He may even have persuaded her that God was telling her to participate in the contest.

That's how Tommy Tenney describes it in his historical-fiction novel *Hadassah: One Night with the King*. When Esther wonders whether she's defiling herself by sleeping with a man to whom she isn't married, Mordecai convinces her that she isn't, that she has no choice, and he even compares her situation to Rebekah's, for whom God arranged a marriage! Instead, he exhorts Esther to go to the king's chamber and "not to act reluctantly or sullenly."[18]

I can truly imagine that such a conversation took place, that Mordecai believed his own words, for it's so easy to deceive ourselves when we're overcome with fear. Mordecai doesn't seem to have the strength of his ancestors. Unlike Daniel, who was like a strong tree standing tall as immoral winds blew, Mordecai bends in the wind. D. Rowlands comments that Esther married a heathen, which the Jews were forbidden to do; she became a concubine before she became a wife; and she resorted to duplicity. In reply to the argument that disobedience would bring death, Rowlands writes, "Death is better than dishonour."[19]

Review Esther 2:12–14.

18. Describe the preparation for the night with the king.

19. How long did each virgin spend with the king?

20. After her night with the king, where did she go?

21. Which girls would see the king again?

22. According to Frederic William Bush, the Hebrew idiom that means "to go to," "went in to," or "came to" is "a frequently used OT euphemism for sexual intercourse.... (The NIV actually translates this idiom as "go sleep with.") Given the frequency with which it is used here, it may well be used with a double entendre."[20] How is this idiom used in the following Scriptures?

   A. Genesis 16:2

B. Ruth 4:13

C. 2 Samuel 11:4

23. Now find this same idiom in Esther 2:12–14. (Hint: It occurs four times in this passage.) What light does this shed on what was happening here?

24. Joyce Baldwin says that this account reveals "the inhumanity of polygamy" and that although the twelve months of beauty treatments were akin to marriage preparation, "the sad part is that for the majority what awaited them was more like widowhood than marriage."[21] How do you think you would feel if you were one of the many who was never called for again?

Review Esther 2:15–18.

25. Whose advice did Esther follow concerning how to adorn herself? (v. 15) Why do you think she did this?

26. How did those who saw her respond to her? (v. 15) How did Xerxes respond? (v. 17)

27. Describe the coronation banquet of Esther. (vv. 17–18)

28. Sit quietly before God and ask Him to show you whether you are "off mission" in any area of your life. Do you sense that He is calling you to make a U-turn and come back into the center of His will? Write down any thoughts you may have.

Memory Work

Review your memory verses.

DAY 5
• •

Between a Rock and a Hard Place

Is it ever right to do wrong? This is a difficult theological issue, and I'm very aware that I myself will give an account to a holy God for what I teach on this subject.

After years of studying the book of Esther, I don't think that Mordecai and Esther did the right thing in these opening chapters. I also think it's very dangerous to allow ourselves to think that God might lead against His Word. What do you do, however, when you have to choose between two wrongs?

Believers have debated, for example, whether it was right for Brother Andrew to smuggle Bibles into closed countries or for Corrie ten Boom to hide the Jews during World War II. Even more controversial is Dietrich Bonhoeffer's participation in the plot to assassinate Hitler, a decision that eventually led to Bonhoeffer's martyrdom. In my opinion, when God weighs the hearts of these believers at the end of time, they will be honored for their faith—as Rahab and the parents of Moses were (see Heb. 11:23, 31)—and for their unselfish motives in trying to help others. They weren't trying to cling to their own lives as Mordecai and Esther seemed to be, but instead they were risking their lives because they feared God and saw a great wrong being committed against the helpless. Proverbs 24:11–12 reveals God's heart on this:

> *Rescue those being led away to death;*
>
> *hold back those staggering toward slaughter.*
>
> *If you say, "But we knew nothing about this,"*
>
> *does not he who weighs the heart perceive it?*
>
> *Does not he who guards your life know it?*
>
> *Will he not repay each person according to what he has done?*

Some have justified Esther and Mordecai's choices because they resulted in saving God's people from a holocaust. I would agree with D. Rowlands, who cautions us against thinking that their later success justified their earlier actions. If we're going to reason like that, we would have to applaud Joseph's brothers for selling him into slavery or the Jews for demanding that the Savior be crucified.[22]

Yet even when we choose a lower road, God can bring good out of it. God brought good out of the immoral choice of Joseph's brothers and, I believe, out of the immoral choices of Mordecai and Esther. Charles Spurgeon wrote,

> The Scripture does not excuse, much less commend, the wrong doing of Esther and Mordecai in thus acting, but simply tells us how divine wisdom brought good out of evil, even as the chemist distills healing drugs from poisonous plants.[23]

Personally, I find great consolation in the fact that even though Esther and Mordecai failed God, He didn't abandon them. I don't believe that God led them into sin, but it's clear that He was still with them in spite of their wrong choices. He brings beauty out of ashes. That's why we call Him the Redeemer.

When we ourselves have to face hard choices, we must be aware of how easy it is to be deceived by our own hearts. We must remember the holiness of God and the fact that we will one day have to give an account of our choices to Him.

29. What do you learn about God from the following passages?

    A. James 1:13

    B. 1 John 1:5

    C. Psalm 18:24–26

30. According to Jeremiah 17:5–9, why should we not trust in people? Why should we not trust in our own hearts?

    Whom should we trust and why?

31. Briefly describe a time, if any, when you trusted in your own heart and were wrong. What have you learned to keep you from repeating this error?

32. Drawing on the wisdom in the following passages, formulate questions to ask yourself when facing difficult choices.

    A. Psalm 119:9–11

    B. Philippians 4:8

    C. Matthew 22:36–40

    D. 1 Peter 2:19–23

The question "What would Jesus do?" from Charles Sheldon's classic *In His Steps* is helpful when we're faced with a decision of ethics. The glorious light of the life of Christ illumines the darkness of our hearts, the godless counsel of others, and the lies of Satan.

Memory Work

Continue reviewing your memory verses. (Don't forget to review Romans 11:33–36 as well.)

Detective for the Divine

How have you seen God at work in your life in the past twenty-four hours through His Word, His presence, and His provision? (Note any specific answers to prayer.)

What was most memorable about the way God worked in your life this week?

Prayer Time

Gather in groups of two or three and spend several minutes offering "popcorn prayers." (See the following diagram for an example of popcorn prayer.)

Four

His Plans Are Not to Harm Us

W e now approach the day of despair in Esther. In a different day of despair, God told His people through the prophet Jeremiah,

"For I know the plans I have for you," declares the LORD, "plans to prosper you and not to harm you, plans to give you hope and a future." (Jer. 29:11)

So often when we face great pain, we lose hope, fearing that God has forgotten us. Yet His plans for His children are always for good, even though, surprisingly, they usually involve pain and sorrow.

A little over a year before I began revising this guide, my fifty-nine-year-old husband lost his battle with colon cancer. Though I weep daily and sometimes have moments when my sobbing seems uncontrollable, I also know that even though I'm temporarily struck down, I will get up, and that despite intense sorrow, there is, indeed, inextinguishable joy. Despite my frailty and pain, I absolutely know that God is good and His purposes are never to harm me but to give me hope and a future. My children and I have seen evidence upon evidence of His mysterious care in the midst of our grief.

The most dramatic evidence can be seen in a miraculous painting of Aslan (the lion representing Christ from C. S. Lewis's Narnia series) that our daughter Sally completed on the day we received Steve's diagnosis. She wanted to capture Lewis's description that the lion was not safe, but he was good.

Each night that summer she'd come down from her studio, frustrated: "I've got the 'not safe' part, but I can't get the 'good' part." Yet the day Sally completed her painting, we saw another animal that she hadn't intended to paint. At the heart of the lion appeared a lamb that looked as if it had been slain. We thought of the passage in Revelation where John beheld "the Lion of the tribe of Judah," and then he looked again and saw "a Lamb, looking as if it had been slain" (5:5, 6). (You can see the painting and a movie clip of the story by visiting my Web site, www.deebrestin.com.) God knew we would need this reassurance of His love as my husband and the father of our five children suffered and died. Truly, Jesus has been a Lion in our lives, tearing apart our lives as we knew them and tearing away the beloved husband and father from us. But at God's heart, and this we must always remember, is a Lamb who was slain for us. The Lord isn't safe, but He is good. This enormous painting now hangs in my living room—it's my Ebenezer, a sign of God's presence right in the middle of our pain.

In Esther, as the edict for the holocaust against the Jews was announced, there was great mourning among God's people. They didn't know the end of the story, but we do, and we can also see, as they eventually must have, how God never left them. Esther's story contains great evidence of His love, His presence, and His providence—if we'll only look.

Prepare Your Heart to Hear

Before you begin your study each day, be still and know that He is God.

Memory Work

Review Esther 4:12–13 and then continue on with verse 14:

When Esther's words were reported to Mordecai, he sent back this answer: "Do not think that because you are in the king's house you alone of all the Jews will escape."

"For if you remain silent at this time, relief and deliverance for the Jews will arise from another place, but you and your father's family will perish. And who knows but that you have come to royal position for such a time as this?"

WARMUP

Briefly describe a time when you went through great sorrow, yet looking back, you can see evidence that God never left you.

DAY I

Darkness and Despair, Yet God Had a Plan

Although darkness and despair were about to reign in the story of Esther, it's clear that God had a plan that would prevail over the plan of His enemies. As Mordecai sat at the king's gate, he overheard two of the king's officials planning to assassinate Xerxes. Mordecai foiled the assassination attempt and the officials were put to death, but Mordecai wasn't even thanked or rewarded. Yet his good deed was recorded in the chronicles of the king. Years before disaster hit, God was at work.

Review Esther 2:19–23.

    1. Describe what happens in this passage.

       How do you think Mordecai felt when no one thanked him?

    2. When you do something significant for someone and they don't seem to notice, how do you deal with your emotions? What scriptural truths speak to your soul at times like these?

Pastor Woodrow Kroll tells of a missionary who was returning to America after a lifetime of service in Africa. On the same ship was Theodore Roosevelt, who had been in Africa on a big-game hunt. An enormous crowd was at the dock to welcome the president home with banners, a band, and great fanfare. But no one was there to show appreciation for the missionary, who had given his life as a servant under primitive conditions. During his time alone with God, the missionary poured out his feelings about being so unappreciated. Then, in the stillness of his heart, God spoke clearly to him, saying, "You're not home yet."[1]

    3. What do you think God has seen in your life that has pleased Him but that others may not have noticed? (Comfort yourself with these thoughts, but don't share them with the group.)

Detective for the Divine

In what ways have you seen God at work in your life during the past twenty-four hours?

DAY 2
. . . .

The Enemy of God's People

My husband, a Gentile, was adopted by a Jewish family. My mother-in-law used to ask me,

"Dee, you study your Bible. Why have the Jews been so persecuted?"

I could only say that Satan has always plotted against God's people—he comes to kill, steal, and destroy. So often we think we struggle against flesh and blood, but in fact we're engaged in a battle against spiritual enemies in high places. Behind the hate of Haman, behind the hate of Hitler, behind the hate of those martyring believers today is Satan himself. He will not prevail, but he will cause great suffering until God binds him and throws him into a lake of burning sulfur forever.

Even before Esther, God's people had enemies. Haman was an Agagite, a fact repeatedly mentioned in Esther. This is also a crucial clue in understanding the friction between Haman and Mordecai. Again and again in the book of Esther, the narrator identifies Haman as an Agagite and Mordecai as a Jew (and not only a Jew but also a Benjamite and therefore related to Saul).

Read 1 Samuel 15:1–23.

4. What did God tell Saul to do? (v. 3) What did Saul actually do? (v. 9)

5. What did God tell Samuel? (v. 11)

6. How did Saul deceive himself? (v. 13)

7. How did Samuel point out Saul's sin? (vv. 14, 18)

8. What else did Samuel tell Saul? (vv. 22–23)

9. Do you have your own agenda for serving the Lord, or are you truly listening to Him and following His agenda? Explain. (If not, you may, like Saul, be working at cross-purposes with Him.)

10. How does one listen to God and receive His agenda for the day?

Read Esther 3:1–2.

11. What did Xerxes do in verse 1? How do you think Mordecai might have felt about this, since he had been the one to save the king from assassination?

12. How are Mordecai and Haman referred to in Esther 2:5 and 3:1. What do you think the narrator was trying to communicate by referring to them this way?

The narrator "assumed his readers would recognize the tribal and racial enmity implied by the patronymics of the two men."[2]

13. According to verse 2, what did all the king's servants do and why?

14. What did Mordecai refuse to do? What might have been his motivation for disobeying the king's command?

Memory Work

Continue working on your memory verses for this week.

DAY 3

Being Honest with God

Have you ever given a religious reason to avoid doing something you simply didn't want to do? Sometimes when people say, "I'll see how the Lord leads," what they really mean is, "I'll see if I want to do that."

Brennan Manning writes, "The temptation of the age [is] to look good without being good."[3] Our enemy Satan not only works against us, but he also encourages us to deceive ourselves. According to Manning, "The Evil One is the great illusionist. He varnishes the truth and encourages dishonesty."[4]

The question we'll consider today is whether Mordecai's refusal to bow down to Haman was due to religious scruples or ethnic pride. And then after examining Mordecai's motives, we'll turn the light on our own deceitful hearts. How often do we fail to be honest with God?

The reason Mordecai gave for refusing to bow was that he was a Jew. But that reason doesn't seem to measure up to the plumb line of Scripture. First, let's consider what the didactic scriptures have to say.

15. What does each of the following Scriptures teach?

    A. Romans 13:1–2

    B. Titus 3:1

    C. 1 Peter 2:13–17

16. Consider how David behaved before King Saul (1 Sam. 24:4–10). What reason does David give for showing Saul honor?

Some might argue that Mordecai was right to refuse to bow down to Haman, for Scripture makes it clear that only God is worthy of our worship (Ex. 20:4; Rev. 22:8–9). However, bowing can be a way of showing respect, like standing when a person of authority or age enters the room. It's not necessarily indicative of worship. It's also true that even if you don't respect the person in authority, you can still respect the office God ordained. For example, when former president Bill Clinton arrived at the National Prayer Breakfast shortly after he had been involved in a lurid sexual scandal with a young intern, about half of the believers stood and about half refused to stand. I believe they all should have stood, not because of the man, but out of respect for the office God ordained.

Likewise, I believe that Mordecai should have obeyed the king's command and bowed when Haman passed by—not to worship the man but to obey the king and show respect for the office. The narrator doesn't tell us Mordecai's motive, but he implies it by mentioning repeatedly that the Jews and the Agagites were enemies. Frederic Bush says that the repetition of this fact makes it likely that ethnic pride was the motive for Mordecai's refusal to bow.[5] *The Bible Knowledge Commentary* concurs, differentiating worship from showing respect for an office:

Probably this persistent (day after day) refusal stemmed more from pride than from religious scruples. For several years Mordecai had not let Esther tell the king she was a Jewess, but now Mordecai was using their national heritage as an excuse for not giving honor to a high Persian official.[6]

Read Esther 3:3–6.

17. Who noticed that Mordecai was neither bowing down nor paying homage to Haman? (v. 3)

18. What reason did Mordecai give to the king's officials? (v. 4)

19. What was Haman's reaction when he learned of Mordecai's refusal to bow or pay homage? (vv. 5–6) Why do you think he reacted this way?

20. What do you think about the fact that these officials didn't know Mordecai was a Jew even though he had lived among them so long?

21. Would the people in your community or workplace know that you were a Christian without being told? Why or why not?

22. Do you think Mordecai should have bowed to Haman out of respect for the office even though he didn't respect the man himself? Explain.

23. Is it hard for you to respect political leaders who lack integrity? According to 1 Timothy 2:1–4 why should we pray for them?

Now turn the light on yourself and consider how honest you are with God. Let Him search your heart.

24. The last time you were in a Sunday worship service, how honest were you with God in your worship? Did you truly worship Him, or did you just seem to be worshiping? What's your tendency? Explain.

25. The last time you read your Bible, how honest were you with God about wanting to know Him better? Were you truly seeking Him, or were you just reading your Bible to feel good about reading your Bible? What's your tendency? Explain.

26. How honest are you with God about your motives for doing good deeds (e.g., for recognition or praise from people or for praise from God)? Explain. When did you last do a good deed that only God knew about? (Don't share this with the group.)

27. How honest do you feel you are with God about your motives in your day-to-day life? Explain.

Detective for the Divine

How have you seen God at work in your life in the past twenty-four hours?

DAY 4
. . . .

The Edict for the Holocaust

Again in the story of Esther, we see God's hand. Though His people didn't seem to be taking the high road, He didn't forsake them. Even though Haman had determined to annihilate the Jewish people after his conflict with Mordecai, God gave His people time to prepare for the coming holocaust and to pray for redemption.

Read Esther 3:7–9.

28. What did Haman do to determine the time of the planned holocaust of the Jews? What does this action tell you about the beliefs of the Persians?

John Whitcomb believes that Satan was behind the massacre of the Jews in Nazi Germany. Likewise, Whitcomb writes, the "titanic death-struggle of the Book of Esther simply cannot be understood apart from the satanic purposes toward Israel."[7] The practices and superstitions of the ancient Persians—consulting astronomers (see Est.1:13), fearing unlucky numbers, and throwing the pur (casting lots) to make decisions—reveal the hold Satan had on this pagan kingdom. Although the Persians saw the number thirteen as unlucky, they felt bound to follow the lot. Some people are astonished that Haman would have been willing to wait nearly a year to carry out his pogrom (massacre), but Whitcomb explains that in the Near East it would have been unthinkable to ignore the wisdom of the astrologers or magicians. The fact that Haman was in bondage to Satan's wisdom facilitated the ultimate victory of the Jews. Even the time that Haman cast the lot seems significant, for it was the month of Nisan, the time when the Jewish people celebrated Passover to commemorate their miraculous deliverance from slavery in Egypt.[8]

29. Behind Haman's hatred was the Father of Lies. Note the truth, the half-truth, and the bold-faced lie in Haman's speech to Xerxes in 3:8.

30. What request did Haman make of the king in verse 9? How did he sweeten the deal?

The sum Haman proposed was vast, amounting to two-thirds of the annual income of the whole empire, a very welcome offer after Xerxes' expensive defeat in Greece. Esther 3:11 might lead you to believe that Xerxes refused it, but his initial refusal was the beginning of polite Oriental bargaining (see Gen. 23). Later in the story we see that Xerxes did indeed take the money (Est. 4:7; 7:4).

Read Esther 3:12–15.

31. What exactly was the edict? Where was it to be published?

32. How did the people of Susa react to the news?

33. What does the narrator say in verse 15 to highlight the coldheartedness of Haman and Xerxes?

Memory Work

Review your memory verses for this week.

DAY 5

. . . .

Put on the Full Armor of God

We may feel as if we're battling with evil people on earth, but God tells us that our real battle is with Satan. God has given us weapons of warfare, but we must take them out of the closet and put them on, for we are in a war.

Songs of Praise

During your quiet time, sing (or read aloud) "And Can It Be?" and "Greater Is He That Is in Me."

Read Ephesians 6:10–18.

34. Describe each piece of armor we're to put on and what it represents.

35. If Mordecai and Esther had been spiritually armed, how might they have responded differently at the beginning of this story?

36. What evil or painful situation are you facing in your life? What have you learned from Ephesians 6 or today's lesson that might help you?

37. Without naming or blaming, state a painful situation in your life for which you would love the prayer support of your sisters.

Memory Work

Spend several minutes reviewing your memory verses (including Romans 11:33–36).

Detective for the Divine

In what ways have you grown in your understanding of God in the past twenty-four hours?

What was your most exciting Detective for the Divine discovery this week?

Prayer Time

If you study the lives of great Christians down through history, you'll find that a high percentage of them had the habit of praying through the psalms. Many of the psalms address physical enemies, but we can apply these prayers to the spiritual enemies that surround us. Turn to one of the most picturesque psalms in the Psalter—Psalm 18:1–3—and ask someone in the group to read it aloud. Then go around the circle, taking turns, and give each person the opportunity to lift up the need she listed in the last question to be supported by the others.

When you're finished, have someone read Psalm 18:4–6 in closing. Then encourage each woman in the group to give thanks (in a short sentence) for eternal salvation or for another way God saved her from distress. (Give women the freedom to pass.)

Five

Predicament, Privilege, and Providence

The most exciting life is not the safe life but the life that seeks, with its whole heart, to walk according to the Spirit, not the flesh. So often we play it safe, hiding out in the cleft of the rock, afraid to go higher, afraid to even listen to the Spirit's call. But in choosing to play it safe, we miss out on the opportunity to live the most exciting life we could ever imagine, a life that experiences God and leaves a legacy for generations to come. So sometimes our loving God will shove us out of our hiding places and put us in situations where we have no choice but to walk by faith. That's what happened to Mordecai and Esther, and it may very well happen to you as well, for that seems to be a strategy God frequently uses in the lives of His faithless children.

Prepare Your Heart to Hear

Often, music will soften our hearts and help us hear God better. Before you begin this study, sing one of your favorite hymns or praise songs that lift your eyes and heart to Him.

Memory Work

Review Esther 4:12–14 until you're able to repeat it accurately from memory:

> When Esther's words were reported to Mordecai, he sent back this answer: "Do not think that because you are in the king's house you alone of all the Jews will escape. For if you remain silent at this time, relief and deliverance for the Jews will arise from another place, but you and your father's family will perish. And who knows but that you have come to royal position for such a time as this?"

WARMUP

Each of us has been given different opportunities for service. Think about the "hats" God has given you to wear, such as motherhood, ministry, career, and so on. When He gave you the privilege of wearing these hats, what responsibilities was He also giving you? Share one of your hats with the group and describe the God-given responsibilities that you believe accompany it.

DAY 1

Sackcloth and Ashes

Sometimes the consequences of our actions are astonishingly severe. A lost temper can result in the loss of a precious relationship. A careless moment at the wheel can lead to death. Joyce Baldwin urges us to imagine that we are Mordecai, "who by his pigheaded pride or loyalty to principle brought disaster not only on himself but his own race."[1] When Mordecai learned of Haman's holocaust plot, "he tore his clothes, put on sackcloth and ashes, and went out into the city, wailing loudly and bitterly" (Est. 4:1). This may seem melodramatic to us, but it was the way people mourned at that time, and the gravity of this crisis clearly justified such a reaction. In every province the Jews were fasting, weeping, and wailing. Many covered themselves in sackcloth and ashes to express their grief. Although the narrator doesn't comment on the significance of this action, it typically demonstrated a spirit of repentance and supplication.

When Esther heard that Mordecai was mourning at the king's gate, she was alarmed. It would like watching a family member cry out in distress after receiving a phone call. You would be frightened and would want to know the reason for the distress.

Esther sent clothing for Mordecai to put on, probably so that he could enter the palace and talk to her, since he wasn't permitted to enter the king's "merry world" wearing sackcloth and ashes (v. 2).[2]

But Mordecai refused the clothes. Joyce Baldwin sees his refusal as discourteous but that that "it would nevertheless be in keeping with his awkwardness which caused the crisis in the first place.[3]

1. Describe the actions of Mordecai, the Jews, and Esther in this passage.

2. Fasting can be a sign of repentance. Read Jonah 3 and describe the reaction of the Ninevites to Jonah's message. Why did they fast and put on sackcloth? (Support your answer from the text.)

3. What do you think Mordecai may have been feeling, and why?

4. Describe a time, if any, when a sinful or foolish choice you made had enormous negative consequences not only for you but also for others. How did you feel?

What might a wise response and a foolish response to this situation have been? How did you actually respond, and what was the result?

Personal Action Assignment

God is pleased when we repent and take responsibility for the sins of our nation. Spend time confessing your own sins and the sins of your nation to the Lord. Let the following praise song and hymns guide you into a spirit of self-examination and repentance: "Search Me, O God," "Holy, Holy, Holy," and "Have Thine Own Way."

Detective for the Divine

Did you sense God's speaking to you through His Spirit during the personal action assignment? If so, briefly share what He spoke to your heart.

DAY 2

Predicament

Elizabeth Dole has had an admirable life of public service. In addition to serving under five U.S. presidents and most recently as a senator from North Carolina, she has also had the distinction of being only the second woman since Clara Barton to serve as president of the American Red Cross.

In *Finding God at Harvard*, Dole tells of a sermon she heard on Esther by Gordon MacDonald that changed her life, encouraging her not to play it safe but to step out in faith to live for Christ on a day-by-day basis.[4] In his sermon MacDonald highlighted three themes in Esther 4:13–14: predicament, privilege, and providence.

Today we lead up to Mordecai's famous speech in which he persuades Esther to intervene for her people by explaining the enormous predicament they find themselves in. The only way out of this predicament is for Esther to come out of her hiding place and take an enormous risk. She may die if she does what Mordecai asks—but if she doesn't do it, she will surely die.

First, let's look at the historical account and consider the predicament that Mordecai, Esther, and all the Jews find themselves in.

Read Esther 4:5–8.

   5. What did Mordecai tell Hathach? (vv. 7–8)

   6. How long had Esther hidden her faith from Xerxes? (Compare Esther 2:16 with Esther 3:7.) What do you imagine this secrecy involved?

   7. Put yourself in Esther's shoes as she received the report from Hathach and heard Mordecai's request. What feelings do you think she might have had?

   8. Based upon what you already know about Xerxes from this study, would you have agreed to go to him on behalf of your people? (It might help to imagine a similar scenario with Hitler.)

Read Esther 4:9–11.

   9. What did Esther tell Hathach? (v. 11)

   10. How many times did Esther mention the king in her response? What does this tell you about her perspective?

Kings were protected not only from being vexed by people problems but also from assassination attempts. That's why no one could approach without being summoned. Xerxes was, according to historical accounts, eventually assassinated in his bed.

   11. List some possible reasons why Xerxes hadn't summoned Esther for more than thirty days. How do you think Esther may have felt about this?

Read Esther 4:12–14.

   12. Write out Mordecai's famous persuasive speech. (vv. 13–14) Do your best to find the phrases that explain the following. (Hint: They're listed in order.)

     A. Predicament

B. Privilege

C. Providence

Mordecai began his speech by telling Esther that she shared the predicament of the Jews: "Do not think that because you are in the king's house you alone of all the Jews will escape" (v. 13). Elizabeth Dole wrote: "It seems that Mordecai [was] saying, 'If the thing that stops you from being a servant to thousands of people is your comfort and your security, forget it. You are no more secure in there than we are out here.'"[5]

13. How easily we cling to our lives, just as Esther was longing to cling to hers. What did Jesus say in Matthew 16:24–25 to urge us out of our safe cocoons?

What application does this have to your life right now?

Memory Work
Review Esther 4:12–14, making it word perfect.

DAY 3
• •

Privilege

Mordecai continued his speech: "For if you remain silent at this time, relief and deliverance for the Jews will arise from another place, but you and your father's family will perish" (Est. 4:14).

Pastor MacDonald put it like this: "God has given you, Esther, the *privilege* to perform. If you don't use that privilege, He may permit you to be pushed aside and give your role to someone else."[6] Elizabeth Dole realized that if she used her privilege for her own selfish goals, for her own career advancement, and not in submission to God, He might take it from her and give it to someone else. "The fear of the LORD is the beginning of wisdom" not only in salvation, but also in living wholeheartedly for Him (Ps. 111:10).

Songs of Praise

During your personal quiet time, sing (or read aloud) "Living for Jesus."

14. The Old Testament prophets spoke of a remnant of God's people whom He would save from destruction. What might Mordecai have known about this remnant from the following passages?

    A. Isaiah 10:21–22

    B. Micah 2:12

15. What did Mordecai believe God would do to deliver His people if Esther didn't use her privilege for good? What did Mordecai say would happen to her and her family if she refused to intervene? (Est. 4:14)

Most people think Mordecai meant that God could still deliver the Jews through another source but that Esther would lose her privilege to be used. Joyce Baldwin writes,

> God's purposes are not thwarted by the failure of one individual to respond positively to his leading, and the individual is truly free to refuse it, though this leads to loss rather than gain.[7]

God isn't boxed in by a person's disobedience. He may simply take power from a disobedient believer and give it to an obedient believer, as He did when He took the kingship of Israel from Saul and gave it to David.

16. Why isn't God limited by our disobedience? Can you think of an example from Scripture or your own life?

Personal Action Assignment

Consider God's call upon your life. What talents and spheres of influence has He given you? Ask yourself, *Am I taking these privileges seriously? Am I doing what God has called me to do?*

Detective for the Divine

How have you grown in your understanding of God in the past twenty-four hours?

DAY 4

Providence

Finally, Mordecai closed with the clincher: "And who knows but that you have come to a royal position for such a time as this?" (Est. 4:14).

If he meant that God had led Esther to sleep with the king, marry a Gentile, and hide her faith so that she could one day deliver her people from a holocaust, then I would have to disagree with his reasoning, for I'm convinced that God doesn't lead us into sin. However, I absolutely know that God is a Master of bringing beauty out of ashes. Even if we've made a mess of our lives—or if others have made a mess of our lives—He is there, ready to redeem. He is near to the brokenhearted and the contrite in spirit. He was with Esther even though He wasn't the One who led her into this situation. I find great comfort in this not only for victims of abuse but also for myself when I've made a mess of my life. My God is waiting with open arms for His prodigal child, eager to put a robe on my shoulders and to celebrate my U-turn.

I wasn't, for example, a good mother with my firstborn. I was twenty, didn't know the Lord, and didn't know how to set and keep boundaries. Yet three years later, when my toddler was ruling the house, I ran to God as a new believer, and He restored the years the locusts had eaten. Today my son deeply loves and serves the Lord. As I look back, I can see the same themes (predicament, privilege, and providence) that appear in Esther, though in a much more limited scope:

- My predicament was that I had a toddler who was making life miserable for Steve and me (and himself!).
- My privilege was that I had been called to be his mother and to raise him in the ways of the Lord.
- God's providence led me to a godly mother who was able to mentor me.

The hero in Esther and the hero in each of our lives is God. Charles Swindoll writes, "This book is not about ancient Persia, it's about us!"[8]

Review Esther 4:13–14.

17. What do you think Mordecai meant by what he said to Esther at the end of verse 14?

18. How do the following passages show God's working on behalf of His children in difficult situations? What is His purpose?

    A. Isaiah 61:1–3

    B. Romans 8:28–29

19. Think of a difficult situation from your past. (It could have been caused by your own sin or by circumstances beyond your control.) What evidence of God's mercy or hand upon you can you see?

Did any good come out of this situation? Explain.

What, if anything, did you learn that helped you be conformed to the image of Christ?

Memory Work

Continue working on your memory verses for the week.

DAY 5

. . . .

Encouraging Our Children to Be Brave

One mother tells of her son moving his young family to a large Midwestern city where he started his first job as a structural engineer. One of the first projects he was asked to design was an abortion clinic. He called her, letting her know that his brand-new job was on the line if he refused. She empathized with his dilemma, but she knew that he needed her to encourage him to do what was right. She says, "I told him that even if he lost his job for refusing, God would bless him as He had blessed the Hebrew midwives." (See Ex. 1:15–20.) Her son did take a stand, and God gave him favor with his employer. He kept his job and was instead asked to design a different and more exciting project.

Charles Swindoll writes, "As a parent, you have occasions in your life, brief vignettes, little windows of time, where you can step forward and help your children to understand the value of being brave."[9] Even if you aren't a mother, you are still called to be a mentor and to seize opportunities to encourage the younger women in your path to be brave, to walk by faith, and to do what is right, no matter the cost.

20. Based upon what you've learned about Mordecai so far, why was he in a unique position to influence Esther?

21. Why do parents sometimes encourage their children to seek what's comfortable rather than what's brave or right?

22. Review Mordecai's words in Esther 4:13–14. Remembering the themes of predicament, privilege, and providence, imagine that your daughter or a young woman you know is facing one of the following scenarios: (1) deciding whether to follow

through with an unplanned pregnancy, (2) deciding whether to confront an abusive husband, or (3) deciding whether to say yes to a call to the mission field.

Choose one scenario and discuss how you might encourage her to obey the Lord (do the right thing) in this situation, even though it might feel frightening.

23. What do you think you'll remember from today's lesson?

Memory Work

Spend some time reviewing this week's memory verses from Esther as well as Romans 11:33–36.

Detective for the Divine

How have you sensed God at work in your life in the past twenty-four hours through His Word, His presence, and His provision?

What was your best Detective for the Divine discovery this week?

Prayer Time

Cluster in groups of three or four for prayer, using the ACTS acronym to guide you:

A—Adoration (Use some of God's names for inspiration: the Redeemer, the Word, the Light of the World, the Good Shepherd, the Resurrection and the Life.)

C—Confession (Confess your sins to God audibly or silently.)

T—Thanksgiving (Thank God for ways you've seen Him working in your life this week.)

S—Supplication (Lift a personal need to Him and allow the other women in your group to support you with sentence prayers.)

Six

Out of the Cocoon of Crisis Emerges a Butterfly

Five years earlier, Esther was afraid to take a life-or-death stand. Now, with more maturity, with Mordecai's encouragement, and with the faith for which she became famous, Esther takes a deep breath and says,

Go, gather together all the Jews who are in Susa, and fast for me. Do not eat or drink for three days, night or day. I and my maids will fast as you do. When this is done, I will go to the king, even though it is against the law. And if I perish, I perish. (4:16)

When God allows a crisis to come into our lives, it tests our faith in Him. If our faith is genuine, a butterfly will emerge out of the cocoon of crisis. Even if we've really blown it, God can use us mightily when we make a U-turn. Sandra Glahn, one of a handful of female professors at Dallas Theological Seminary, writes:

Despite shaky beginnings, Esther does go on to become a great heroine. And in doing so she proves that even a girl with a past—if she has the courage to follow God—can be used to accomplish great things.[1]

Esther then prepared for what was going to be one of the most successful women's ministries in history. Every Christian woman should take note of this. Whether you are seeking a plan for women's ministry, are concerned about a choice your husband is considering, or are experiencing a challenging situation in your life, listen and learn from Esther.

Prepare Your Heart to Hear

Like Esther and her maidens, purpose in your heart to seek God's face daily.

Memory Work

Over the next two weeks, focus on memorizing Esther 4:15–16:

	TYPE	MOTIVE	RESULT
Deuteronomy 8:2–3			
1 Samuel 1:3–11			
2 Samuel 12:13–23			
Nehemiah 1:3—2:4			
Esther 4:3			
Esther 4:16			
Esther 9:31			
Daniel 1:8–17			
Jonah 3:5–9			
Luke 2:36–38			
Luke 4:2–14			
Acts 13:1–3			

Then Esther sent this reply to Mordecai: "Go, gather together all the Jews who are in Susa, and fast for me. Do not eat or drink for three days, night or day. I and my maids will fast as you do. When this is done, I will go to the king, even though it is against the law. And if I perish, I perish."

WARMUP

Fearful situations can refine us, forcing us to cry out to God for wisdom and the faith to step out of our comfort zones. Briefly share a time when this was true in your life.

DAY I
• •

If You Want to Be Effective in Ministry

When my daughter Sally and her close Christian friends were seniors in their public high school, they had a longing to share the gospel with their peers before they graduated. Inspired by Esther's courage as well as her effectiveness, they decided to study her example and do what she did.

The first thing Esther did was to fast with her maids—and we assume that she also prayed. How wise we are if instead of coming up with our own plan and asking God to bless it, we endeavor to discover *God's* plan. This is vital if we're to experience the power of God. Esther's fast was a total fast: no food or drink for three days. Serious situations call for serious measures. Following Esther's example, Sally and her friends decided to give up lunches for a few days and seek God. (More of this story later.)

Scripture is filled with examples of fasting. Jesus himself fasted and implied that it should be a natural part of our lives (e.g., "When you fast ..." [Matt. 6:16]). Historically, great revivals followed times of fasting and prayer. People like John Wesley, George Whitefield, Martin Luther, John Calvin, John Knox, Jonathan Edwards, Andrew Murray, and many more fasted regularly to draw upon God's wisdom and power and to ask for the fires of revival to sweep across their land.

Songs of Praise

Begin your quiet time by meditating on Isaiah 61:3. Then sing "Spirit of the Living God" and "Immortal, Invisible."

1. Read the following Scriptures and see if you can discern the type, motive, and possible result of each fast. Most of these will be normal fasts (water, but no food), but a few may be partial fasts (abstinence from some foods) or total fasts (no food or water). You may need to look at the surrounding context as well. If your time is short, read only the passages with stars. (The fast in Deuteronomy 8:2–3 is the only involuntary fast.)

2. Summarize what these Scriptures have taught you about fasting.

Fasting and prayer almost always occur together in Scripture. Therefore, even though prayer isn't mentioned in Esther, most commentators believe it occurred. Because the account in Esther is so restrained, we're not told specifically why the Jews fasted, but by comparing the fasts in Esther with similar fasts in Scripture, we can gain some insight into the possible reasons.

The fast of the Jews in Esther 4:3 was surely a fast of mourning, but it may also have been a fast of repentance, for the description is similar to the fast of the Ninevites in Jonah. The fast in Esther 4:16 is reminiscent of Nehemiah's fast when he needed God's wisdom and grace before he approached the king. Certainly, Esther needed this as she approached her temperamental and capricious husband. How would Xerxes react? He hadn't shown any interest in her in more than thirty days. He had dethroned (and perhaps executed) the last queen who resisted him. Still, Esther planned to go to him without being summoned, tell him what she had hidden from him all these years, and plead with him to do something about the terrible decree he had signed. If it didn't go well, Esther and all of her people would die. It was an enormous and frightening challenge and so she began with a three-day fast. The final fast in Esther 9:31 was a commemorative fast to help the Jews remember how God turned their mourning into joy when the king granted Esther's request.

My daughter Sally and her friends also wanted God's wisdom so they would know how to effectively reach their high-school friends for Christ. After skipping lunches and praying, they heard that Campus Crusade was bringing the *Jesus* movie to our town during Holy Week. When they heard this, they all came up with the same idea. (The same Spirit often says the same thing to different people at the same time. It's a wonderful way to receive confirmation!) They decided they would go to their principal and ask him if they could have a special showing of the movie in the high-school auditorium the following Saturday and put up posters in the halls and flyers on the students' cars to advertise the event. When Sally told me this, I said, "Sally, how do you possibly think that your principal will agree? This is a public high school!"

Sally looked surprised. "Mom! You've been telling me about Esther and how God granted her favor. Dr. K. is so much nicer than Xerxes. Don't you think God can do the same thing for us?"

I thought, *Yes, this is what I've been telling her*. Still, I couldn't imagine that Dr. K. would agree. So I asked Sally, "How do you plan to approach Dr. K.?"

"We're going to give up a few more lunches, and then we'll draw straws on Friday. Whoever gets the shortest straw has to go to the principal's office and make an appointment with Dr. K. Esther didn't tell Xerxes what she wanted right away, so we won't tell Dr. K. right away. We'll just make the appointment and then give time for God to work on his heart." (To be continued ...)

A fast can help you concentrate so that you can put aside the temporal to seek the eternal. A large part of our lives as women may revolve around the preparation of food, so a fast can help us concentrate on something other than food. It isn't enough, however, to just abstain from food; we must seek the face of God.

3. What warnings and promises can you find concerning false and true fasts in the following passages?

A. Isaiah 58

B. Joel 2:12–14

Detective for the Divine

How have you seen God at work in your life in the past twenty-four hours?

DAY 2

....

And If I Perish, I Perish

Flying home from Thailand with our new twelve-year-old daughter, our fifth child, my husband, Steve, began to talk longingly of the other children we had seen in Bangkok's orphanage for handicapped children. He said, "Some of those little boys were so cute."

Panic began to rise in me. How could I help my husband understand that I had reached my quota of children, at least for now? A word picture! I thought for a moment and then said, "Honey, please imagine that I'm holding on to the airplane wing, clinging by my fingers, praying that I won't slip. I want to keep up with you in your Christian walk, but I'm afraid I'll plummet to my death."

Steve was quiet, absorbing the picture. Then he put his arm around me and asked, "Dee, is that really how you're feeling?"

I nodded and said, "I'm afraid. I don't see how I can adopt more children and survive. But I also want you to know I've given my whole life to the Lord, and if He wants me to adopt more children, then I will....

"And if I perish, I perish."

We laughed, and yet that dramatic line did help communicate my need for support.

Usually we don't perish when we step out into the center of God's will. Usually what we discover is that the road is hard, but God is right there with us. However, unless we're willing to perish, unless we're willing to risk everything to obey God, He won't be able to use us mightily. Pastor Woodrow Kroll once said, "I have never known God to fruitfully use anyone who does not come to the 'If I perish, I perish' understanding of life."[2]

"If I perish, I perish" are the words for which we remember Esther. When a crisis comes into our lives, we discover what we're made of. The cocoon of crisis revealed a beautiful butterfly in Esther's case.

71

Songs of Praise

During your quiet time, sing (or read) "In My Life, Lord."

Read Esther 4:15–17.

4. Meditate on this passage, then answer the following journalists' questions: *Who? What? When? Where? Why? How?*

5. What stood out to you from the previous exercise and why?

6. What was the attitude of the people in the following Scriptures? How did God use them because of it?

   A. Esther 4:16

   B. Daniel 3:17–18

   C. Matthew 26:36–42

   D. Acts 4:13–21; 5:27–29

7. According to Matthew 16:25–26, what attitude are we to have?

8. Summarize the "If I perish, I perish" attitude.

9. Do you have this attitude in life? Explain. (Think about situations in your life that might reveal whether you have this attitude. Consider, for example, not only persecution but the cost that might be involved in obeying a call of God in your career, your marriage, etc.)

Memory Work

Spend a few minutes memorizing Esther's famous speech (Est. 4:15–16).

Passage	Teaching	Esther's Situation
Psalm 32:8		
Proverbs 16:7		
Proverbs 21:1		
Ecclesiastes 4:9–10		
Isaiah 40:31		

DAY 3

Approaching the Dragon One Step at a Time

Charles Swindoll notes that between Esther 4 and 5 is "white space," a "grand pause" of time.[3] During this time of waiting on God, He pours out His wisdom on Esther, for she obviously has a plan and strength from above.

Esther's approach is masterful. She was diplomatic and unrushed. Some think she hesitated because she lost courage. Though she may have been afraid, I don't think that was the reason for her hesitation. I think it was her plan all along to do this slowly, to build suspense, to arouse the king's curiosity. She was walking by faith, one step at a time. In *Taming the Dragons*, Brenda Wilbee writes,

> When the king held out his golden scepter, she did not immediately fall to her knees and beg for mercy. She approached this dragon one step at a time, asking only for what she felt capable of obtaining.[4]

Read Esther 5:1–8.

10. Record the steps Esther took in the following passages:

A. Esther 4:16

B. Esther 5:1

      C. Esther 5:2

      D. Esther 5:3–4

      E. Esther 5:6–8

Note that "by the end of her speech Esther has been able to represent what she wants as a matter of 'doing what the king has said' (verse 8), as though it were she rather than he who was doing the favour."[5]

11. What do you learn from the following Scriptures about handling difficult situations? How are these principles illustrated in Esther's situation?

12. What encouragement does Esther's story give you? How can you apply what you've learned to your life?

Detective for the Divine

How have you seen God at work in your life in the past twenty-four hours through time spent in His Word or in prayer?

DAY 4

When You Sense Your Husband Is Going to Make a Serious Mistake

Pastor David Jeremiah, on his national radio program *Turning Point*, advised wives to consider Esther's approach when they think their husbands might be about to make a big mistake. Referring to Esther, Dr. Jeremiah said,

> She had to go and tell him that what he was about to do was wrong.... In that culture you did not confront your husband about anything ... especially if he happened to be king.... She had a well-thought-out plan ... she fasted and prayed ... she didn't run into the king's court and just give him a piece of her mind.... She sought the Lord to intervene for her ... she put on her prettiest dress.... She waited for the appropriate moment. (Don't try to approach your husband when he is hungry, tired, or in a hurry—or when you are angry.) ... She put together a gourmet meal....

> Notice how she asks the question: "If I have found favor, if it pleases the king" (Esther 5:7). Here's the translation: "If you think it would be all right Sweetheart, and if you like the idea, could you please?"

74

She implored him with tears ... genuine tears....

There is a way to approach your husband when you sense he's going in the wrong direction. The whole key to success was her attitude.[6]

I so appreciated Dr. Jeremiah's message, for too often I feel that the Scriptures are distorted, making wives feel they should do nothing and let their husbands make serious mistakes. Although I do agree that we shouldn't nag or manipulate, we must, as coheirs in the gospel of grace, speak the truth in love. That's exactly what Esther did.

13. Describe Esther's attitude in approaching her husband in the following passages. Look carefully at each scenario and see what you can discover. Then imagine that you're in a similar scenario with a husband, boss, or other authority figure. What can you learn from Esther?

   A. Esther 4:15–16

   B. Esther 5:4

   C. Esther 8:3–6

14. Let's consider two other accounts of women who thought their husbands were making a mistake: Abigail, who was married to an unbeliever, a fool; and Sarah, who was married to Abraham, a giant of the faith. Read each account and see what you can glean from how these women approached two very different kinds of husbands, whom these women thought were making big mistakes.

   A. Review the story of Abigail and Nabal in 1 Samuel 25. What mistake did Abigail feel Nabal was making?

   Why didn't she talk to him about her plans?

   What catastrophe did she avoid?

   How did God deal with Nabal?

   B. Read the account of Sarah and Abraham in Genesis 21. What mistake did Sarah feel Abraham had made? (Ironically, he had made this mistake with her help!)

   What did Sarah say to Abraham? Why do you think Sarah spoke to her husband about this?

How did God deal with Abraham, as well as Hagar and her son?

C. What key principles do you learn from the examples of Esther, Abigail, and Sarah that can help you approach your husband (or someone else in authority) when you think he's making a mistake?

D. What differences, if any, do you see between the three women and their approaches? What do you think accounts for these differences?

Memory Work

Polish your memory verses.

DAY 5

How Not to Approach Your Husband: The Story of Zeresh

As women, we're knit together with those we love, and when they hurt, we hurt. If someone hurts my child, my husband, or my dear sister in Christ, I can react like a mother bear. Zeresh shows us how dangerous this is!

Ruthie Thune, wife of the senior pastor of Christ Community Church in Omaha, told me that the book of Esther has made her more aware of her influence over her husband. She told me,

> Sometimes Bob will come home from a church board meeting mildly upset. One of the members has been critical of him or the church. As Bob's main sounding board, I realize that the way I react will have a tremendous impact not only on him but on the whole church. If I believe the member's words have merit, I can gently stimulate Bob to consider them carefully. If I become angry, I contribute strength to Bob's initial resistance. So I'm keenly aware of my need to be sensitive to God's still small voice.

15. How do you feel when someone hurts or upsets a loved one?

Read Esther 5:9–14.

16. What did Mordecai do (or not do) that enraged Haman? (v. 9)

17. List (in order) the things Haman boasted about to his wife and friends. (vv. 11–12)

What was the fly in the ointment that kept Haman from enjoying his vast wealth and influence? (v. 13)

18. How did Zeresh respond to her husband's grievances? (v. 14)

What was foolish about her response?

19. What can you learn from the example of Zeresh about foolish and dangerous ways to respond?

How can you apply this to your own life?

Memory Work

Spend the next few minutes reviewing Esther 4:12–16 and Romans 11:33–36. Repeat them a few times until you can say them more smoothly.

Detective for the Divine

Has God shown you special mercy in the past twenty-four hours? If so, how?

What was your most meaningful Detective for the Divine discovery this week?

Prayer Time

Pair off in twos and pray together.

Seven

"If God Is for Us, Who Can Be Against Us?"

Remember the story I was telling you about my daughter and her friends? We were at the point in the story where they were going to approach the principal about showing the *Jesus* movie at their school. When they drew straws to see who would represent them, Sally drew the shortest straw. So she went to the principal's office to talk with Dr. K. This was their conversation:

Dr. K.: "Come in, Sally! How can I help you?"

Sally: "I need to talk to you about something very important, Dr. K. Could I schedule an appointment for Monday?"

Dr. K.: "You can talk to me right now, Sally. This is a good time. Sit down."

Sally: "I'm sorry, sir. I need to wait until Monday."

Dr. K.: "What's this about, Sally?"

Sally: "I can tell you everything on Monday, Dr. Kenagy."

Dr. K. smiled, his eyebrow raised in curiosity: "Okay, Sally. I'll see you at eight o'clock on Monday morning."

Sally left his office encouraged, wondering what God would do before Monday and praying that He would, indeed, do something!

And He did. Sally was a member of a high-school choral group called the Madrigals. The group was going to be in an important concert that Saturday at the state capital in Lincoln, Nebraska, which was two hours away. So Sally decided to drive down Friday night to stay with her brother and sister-in-law.

When she arrived at her brother's house, she realized she'd forgotten her long black dress and called Dr. K.'s daughter, Katie, to ask for help. (Katie was also in the group.) She knew that Katie's dad would have all the keys to the high school, including the choir room where Sally's dress was. So she asked if Katie and her dad could pick up her dress on their way to the concert.

When Katie talked to her dad, he was very gracious, saying, "I'll go over right now and get it so we don't forget."

But the next morning, even though he had the dress, he *still* forgot it. Just as the events in Esther seemed to be engineered by an unseen hand, that morning a series of events contributed to Dr. K. and Katie forgetting the dress: Katie overslept, it was snowing, and Dr. K. was concerned they'd be late. So they rushed out of the house, leaving Sally's dress behind. When Katie and her dad arrived, Sally came running out to thank them. Dr. K. blanched. How would Sally be able to participate in the concert without a dress? Sally said later, "Even then I could see God's hand. It was an awkward situation, but I had bought a green prom dress the afternoon before, so I wore that. I did stick out like a sore thumb. Everybody kept expecting me to step forward and do a little solo, but I never did. I was just the girl in green with the red face."

Dr. K. left three messages on our answering machine apologizing and saying how gracious Sally had been despite the embarrassing situation. It was clear that he truly felt bad.

When Sally walked into his office on Monday morning, he said, "Whatever you want, Sally, it's yours."

Movie posters went up all over that public high school—and flyers on the cars. The next Saturday the *Jesus* movie was shown to hundreds of students, and dozens of them placed their trust in Christ and signed up for Bible studies the girls had set up on the gospel of John.

If God is for us, who can be against us?

Prepare Your Heart to Hear

Ask God to speak to you in a personal way each day this week (perhaps through a Bible passage or a word of encouragement from another believer). Remember, "He is there and He is not silent."

Memory Work

Work on perfecting Esther 4:15–16:

Then Esther sent this reply to Mordecai: "Go, gather together all the Jews who are in Susa, and fast for me. Do not eat or drink for three days, night or day. I and my maids will fast as you do. When this is done, I will go to the king, even though it is against the law. And if I perish, I perish."

WARMUP

God worked in the heart of Xerxes when he wasn't able to sleep. Has God ever spoken to you during a time of insomnia or through a dream? Briefly share your experience.

DAY 1

"Aslan Is on the Move"

In the Narnia series by C. S. Lewis, Aslan represents Jesus, and he comes to a land where the White Witch reigns and it's always winter but never Christmas. When he arrives, the snow begins to melt, the crocuses appear, and everyone knows that "Aslan is on the move."[1]

In the same way, we clearly see Aslan on the move in the climax of the story in Esther. The excitement began in Esther 5 and now escalates. The chapters that follow are filled with evidences of God on the move.

Read Esther 6.

> 1. Based upon the example for Esther 6:1–3, describe each of the following scenes as if it were a scene in a play. Use your imagination for details and emotions.
>
> A. Esther 6:1–3

Xerxes, reclining in his royal bed of purple satin, listens to a eunuch drone on from the book of the chronicles. Suddenly the eunuch reads about a foiled assassination attempt. Xerxes sits straight up, demanding to know what has been done for the man who saved his life. When told, "Nothing," an organ plays chords of suspense.

> B. Esther 6:4–10

> C. Esther 6:11

> D. Esther 6:12–14

In *The Lion, the Witch and the Wardrobe,* as the White Witch flees in her sleigh with her captive, Edmund, a problem occurs. A thaw. Edmund begins to hope that the Witch will be foiled.

> Every moment the patches of green grew bigger and the patches of snow grew smaller. Every moment more and more of the trees shook off their robes of snow....
>
> Soon there were more wonderful things happening. Coming suddenly round a corner into a glade of silver birch trees Edmund saw the ground covered in all directions with little yellow flowers—celandines....

"This is no thaw," said the Dwarf, suddenly stopping. "This is spring. What are we to do? Your winter has been destroyed, I tell you! This is Aslan's doing."

"If either of you mention that name again," said the Witch, "he shall instantly be killed."[2]

There's no doubt in my mind that all of the holocausts planned against the Jews throughout history have been engineered by Satan. Here again, we see his oft-used devices: He hates, he lies, and he plans evil. But Esther and her people had fasted and prayed, and now they are seeing signs of spring! God was on the move.

Review Esther 6:1–11.

2. How do you see God on the move in Esther 6:1–3?

What spiritual parallel do you find in Malachi 3:16?

3. How do you see God on the move in Esther 6:4–5?

4. What wrong assumption did Haman make in verse 6? Describe his suggestion for "the man the king delights to honor." (v. 7)

Haman not only assumed that the king wanted to honor him above everyone else, but according to J. Vernon McGee, "the true nature of Haman is revealed in his answer.... Haman had his eye upon the throne. It was his intention, when the time was right, to eliminate the king."[3]

5. What evidence in this passage tells you that Haman desired the praise of man instead of the praise of God?

6. Whose praise do you desire? (Support your answer with an example.)

Haman, humiliated, rushed home to find comfort in the arms of his wife, and she promptly told him that he was finished! It was foolish, she said, to stand against the Jews! (She must have forgotten that she was the one who suggested a gallows be built for "that Jew Mordecai" [Est. 5:13].)

Joyce Baldwin writes,

> Behind this cold comfort there seems to lie commonly accepted folk wisdom, perhaps proverbial. The way the Jewish people had survived deportations and preserved their identity had not escaped notice, and this in itself witnessed to the power of their God.[4]

7. Compare Zeresh's response to Haman in Esther 5:14 with her response in 6:13. How much time had passed since her first response? What do you think accounts for such a dramatic change?

8. What qualities do you see in Zeresh that you wouldn't want to imitate as a wife?

9. As Joyce Baldwin indicates, God's deliverance of the Jews throughout history could not have gone unnoticed by the surrounding nations. Haman's wife clearly seems to have realized that her husband was fighting a losing battle against God's people. What do the following passages say about the Jewish people and how we should respond to them?

    A. Genesis 12:2–3

    B. Psalm 122:6–9

Detective for the Divine

In what ways have you experienced God's presence and provision during the past twenty-four hours?

DAY 2
. . . .

I Will Curse Those Who Curse You

Do you remember in Esther 3:8 when Haman told Xerxes: "It is not in the king's best interest to tolerate [the Jews]"? What a lie! Now, as the story continues, we see God rushing to defend His persecuted people. Those who touch the apple of God's eye will pay dearly.

10. Read Esther 7-8 and describe the ongoing drama. Watch for dark comedy (comedy dealing with subjects not usually considered funny, such as death, war, and misery.)

    A. Esther 7:1–6

    B. Esther 7:7–9

    C. Esther 7:10

    D. Esther 8:1–6

11. Some might have thought that God's hand of protection wasn't on the Jews beyond the borders of Israel. What does Malachi 1:1–5 teach?

12. What message is delivered through the dark comedy in these chapters?

13. Though many Jewish people have hardened their hearts and refused to accept Jesus as their Messiah, God isn't finished with them yet.

   A. According to Romans 11:1–11, has God rejected His people? Have they stumbled beyond recovery? Explain.

   B. What good thing has come out of the unbelief of the Jews? (Rom. 11:11)

   C. What warning and hope does God give to both Jews and Gentiles in Romans 11:17–24?

14. In what ways have you seen God on the move in your life?

Memory Work

Work on perfecting your memory verses.

DAY 3
. . . .

Grant Me My Life

Eloquent, diplomatic, and discerning, the beautiful Esther finally made her plea to the king. Xerxes repeated that she could ask for as much as half of his kingdom, but instead, she astonished him by pleading for her life and the life of her people!

What is this? he must have thought. *She's the queen, not some common criminal! What is she talking about?*

Then Esther clarified her request by telling the king just how diabolical Haman's plot was: "[We] have been *sold* for destruction and slaughter and annihilation" (Est. 7:4, emphasis added). She added that if her people had just been sold as slaves, she wouldn't have disturbed the king, but since they had been sold for slaughter, she had to plead for their lives.

Read Esther 7:1–6.

15. What does the timing of Esther's request tell you about her skill in knowing how to approach her husband?

16. Earlier in the story, Esther used the third person to address the king—"If it pleases the king ... let the king ... come to a banquet I have prepared for *him*" (Esther 5:4, emphasis added). Now she uses the second person—"You, O king" (7:3). Why do you think she did this?

17. Which of the king's words did Esther repeat in verse 3? Do you think it was wise to repeat his words? Explain.

18. By using the two different words the king used ("petition" and "request"), Esther made it seem as if the king had granted her two favors. What was her petition? What was her request?

19. What words did Esther use to reveal the depravity of Haman's plot? (v. 4) Since these words mean essentially the same thing, why do you think she used all of them?

20. Where did she place the blame? (v. 6) Where was she careful not to place the blame?

21. What can you learn from Esther about gentle persuasion?

22. On a spiritual parallel, Esther had only recently been awakened to the peril that faced her. Likewise, many people today feel comfortable, secure, and unaware of God's wrath and the coming day of judgment. They've been taken captive by the Enemy (Satan) and are headed toward a worse fate than their slavery on earth. What are some ways you can help others become aware of the wrath to come?

Detective for the Divine

How have you seen God in your life in the past twenty-four hours through His Word, His presence, and His provision?

DAY 4

• •

More of God's Fingerprints

Haman's only hope was Esther, and while Xerxes paced the garden in a rage, Haman began pleading with her. When Xerxes returned, Haman was falling onto the queen's couch, and the king accused Haman of molesting his wife.

David J. A. Clines writes,

> It simply strains credulity to believe that [Xerxes] actually thought that Haman under these circumstances was really attempting to assault the queen. Rather, he chooses so to interpret Haman's action, thereby providing a charge with which to condemn him that relieves the king from raising publicly the true reason for the condemnation, the plot against the Jews. Thus, in keeping with the irresponsibility that has consistently marked Ahasuerus' (Xerxes') character, he can leave hidden and unexamined his own complicity in the matter. Another remarkable coincidence has acted in favor of the Jews.[5]

Read Esther 7:7—8:2.

23. How do you see God on the move in this passage?

24. For what crime was Haman executed? What irony do you see in this?

25. What else does Esther reveal to the king in verse 8:1?

Author Joy Dawson observed that neither Esther nor Mordecai could have made it through this crisis alone. She likens them to being on either end of a seesaw, where both partners need to be moving, adding their weight. Dawson exhorts us to be alert to the "ministry link" when God gives us a friend, because He may have a sovereign purpose for bringing this person across our path.[6]

26. Think about your closest friends, your husband, or an adult child, and consider whether there might be a "ministry link." Be still before God for a few moments and write down any thoughts you have.

27. How are the tables completely turned in 8:1–2?

Memory Work

Continue working on your memory verses.

DAY 5

How Can I Bear to See Disaster Fall on My Family?

Esther had asked for her life and the life of her people in chapter 7, but Xerxes was so preoccupied with the life of the queen that he hadn't said anything about saving her people. Taking nothing for granted, Esther returned to the king, this time weeping, falling at his feet, pleading once more for her people.

Again, the king extended the gold scepter to Esther, the sign of favor, and listened to her carefully as she yet again diplomatically asked for something that had never been done before: She wanted the laws of the Medes and Persians overturned. Then she ended her request with these heartrending words: "For how can I bear to see disaster fall on my people? How can I bear to see the destruction of my family?" (Esther 8:6).

The spiritual parallel here brings me to tears. I'm so thankful that God has granted me my petition and given me my life. I'm so thankful to have been rescued from the wrath to come. But I return to the Lord again and again, falling before Him, pleading for the lives of my loved ones who don't know Him and seem unconcerned about the wrath to come. "How can I bear to see disaster fall on my people? How can I bear to see the destruction of my family?"

Since the original writing of this guide, both of my parents have gone to be with the Lord. I didn't have the assurance that either my dad or my mother knew the Lord until shortly before their deaths. But God did a miraculous work in each of their lives. At the age of ninety-three, just months before God took her home, my mother asked my son to help her put her trust in Christ. Quite honestly, even though I had tearfully pleaded with the Lord to bring my parents to faith in Him, I had nearly given up hope. But God responded to me as He responded to Esther, granting life for death, beauty for ashes. I'm overcome with gratitude for His amazing grace.

We have an enemy more powerful than Haman, more dangerous than Hitler. Our enemy the Devil "prowls around like a roaring lion looking for someone to devour" (1 Peter 5:8). Should we not come before the King of Kings and pray for protection? Should we not intercede, with tears, for those Satan seeks to devour?

Songs of Praise

During your personal quiet time, sing one of the following: "Great Is Thy Faithfulness," "Amazing Grace," or "And Can It Be?"

Read Esther 8:3–8.

28. Why did Esther go back to the king? What did she ask for?

29. What is the spiritual parallel for us?

30. What do you learn about effective intercessory prayer from the following passages?

   A. Psalm 51:10–14

   B. Luke 18:1–8

Personal Quiet Time

Spend some time in prayer, interceding for unsaved friends and family. Write down the date, the person's name, and your prayer in a prayer journal or in the back of this guide. The following Scriptures may help guide your prayers: Esther 8:6; 2 Timothy 2:23–26; 1 Peter 3:1–17.

Memory Work

Spend some time reviewing your memory verses, including Romans 11:33–36.

Detective for the Divine

How have you seen God at work in your life in the past twenty-four hours through His Word, His presence, and His provision?

What have you discovered in this lesson that you think might have a lasting impact on your life and the lives of your loved ones?

Prayer Time

Pair off in twos and intercede for your loved ones.

Brothers & Wife

Eight

Sorrow into Joy

As I mentioned earlier, the book of Esther is controversial because the story is relayed without editorial commentary. So we're left to wrestle with these questions:

- ✪ Why is the story of Esther told with such restraint?
- ✪ Why is God's name not mentioned?
- ✪ When we're told that the Jews fasted, why aren't we told whether they also prayed?
- ✪ Should Vashti have obeyed her husband and gone to his drinking party?
- ✪ Should a woman ever defy her husband?
- ✪ Should Esther have hidden her faith?
- ✪ Should she have slept with the king?
- ✪ Should she have married a pagan?
- ✪ Does God ever lead us into sin?
- ✪ Should Mordecai have bowed to Haman?
- ✪ Is it ever right to show respect for an immoral leader?

I've shared the views of respected commentators on all of these questions, and I've encouraged you to hold up each view to the light of Christ and His Word. We should be like the Bereans, who were of "noble character" and "examined the Scriptures every day to see if what Paul said was true" (Acts 17:11). Be wary of modeling your behavior after the behavior of other believers; instead, always ask, "What would Jesus do?"—or perhaps more accurately, "What would Jesus have me do?"

Now we come to another challenging and controversial section. Did Mordecai and Esther go too far with their enemies? Were they outside of God's will when they went beyond defending themselves to destroying and plundering those who opposed them? Again, because there is no editorial commentary, we must consider other passages in Scripture to give us insight into these questions. This also gets into an area where people who deeply love the Lord may have different and strongly held opinions. I've found it interesting that evangelical believers in the United States tend to be quite militaristic in their views, whereas believers in other parts of the world seem to be more open to considering views that differ from their own. For this reason, it's vital that we immerse ourselves in God's Word and cry out to Him for His heart on how to deal with conflict and how to pray for our leaders.

Even when we find that we can't agree on the gray issues, we should treat one another with respect and love. In Romans 14, Paul addressed the believers who were arguing about disputable matters. He reminded each of them that they would give an account to God for their choices (v. 12), and so they needed to be "fully convinced" in their own minds (v. 5). He also exhorted them to "make every effort to do what leads to peace and to mutual edification" (v. 19).

In the final discussion this week, may God give you wisdom and fill you with grace for your sisters, who may see any of these issues differently than you do. And may He give us all listening ears and pure hearts.

Prepare Your Heart to Hear

Ask God to give you His discernment as you study each day's lesson.

Memory Work

Review Romans 11:33 and Esther 4:12–16. I would also encourage you to review these passages each year during Holy Week (the week of Purim, when Haman threw the Pur [cast the lot], the week of Passover, and the week of Easter). If you do this, you'll have them hidden in your heart forever (see Ps. 119:11).

WARMUP

What have you found most controversial in the story of Esther up to this point? How did you resolve the controversy in the light of Christ and His Word? (If you haven't resolved it yet, what steps are you taking to reach a resolution?)

DAY 1

Loving One Another When We're Faced with Disputable Issues

The day before my husband died, he asked me to pick up an absentee ballot for him. It was just before the presidential election in which Republican George W. Bush was given a second term, defeating his Democratic opponent, John Kerry. President Bush and

Senator Kerry held strong, opposing views on the war in Iraq.

Later that day Steve's dearest male friend and medical partner David Wiebe stopped by to visit. David is a strong believer of Mennonite background who grew up on the mission field in India. (The Mennonites have a long history of pacifism.) Because Steve was so very weak, he said to David, "Fill out the ballot for me, brother. I trust you."

So David filled out the ballot. But when it came to the candidate for president, he said, "I need to hear from you, Steve."

Steve hesitated. He truly believed there were more effective ways of combating terrorism than war, but he was also opposed to abortion. Steve felt caught between a rock and a hard place with these two candidates, each of whom was doing something he didn't support. Finally he whispered to David, "Bush."

David was shocked because he and Steve had talked and prayed so much about the war in Iraq. When David came out of Steve's room, he was clearly shaken. Looking at me he said, "Steve asked me to mark the ballot for Bush."

"Did you?" I asked.

"Yes," David said with tears in his eyes.

I could see how much David was hurting, but he was going to do what his dying brother asked him to do. It was a beautiful picture of brothers loving one another despite their political differences. "For now we see through a glass, darkly" (1 Cor. 13:12 KJV), and we may indeed be wrong. But God "looks at the heart" (1 Sam. 16:7), and I know the hearts of both of these men were good, longing to please the Lord.

Before we look at the final chapters of Esther, let's consider how God would have us handle disputable issues and how He would have us treat one another in the process.

Songs of Praise

During your quiet time, sing one or two of these songs about God's power: "Shout to the Lord," "What a Mighty God We Serve," "Jehovah-Jireh, My Provider" or the "Hallelujah Chorus." (If you feel comfortable, go where no one can see you and dance before the Lord like David did.)

Read Romans 14:1–13.

1. What two commands are given in verse 1 concerning a brother "whose faith is weak?"

   accepting Judgement

R. C. Sproul writes, "There must be charity toward the 'weak' brothers whose conscience is still bound by scruples from which the gospel normally sets us free."[1] In light of Romans 14:1, what are some ways you can show love and acceptance for someone who has such scruples?

2. According to verse 2, what gray issue or disputable matter were the Roman believers struggling with?

what they eat

3. What command did Paul give to both the weak and the strong? (v. 3) What reason did he give for accepting each other?

4. What question did Paul ask in verse 4? What answer did he give?

5. What disputable issue is described in verse 5? What command is given to both men?

6. According to verse 6, what does Paul say we all have in common, regardless of our differences?

7. What truth is stated in verse 7? (Try to put it in your own words.)

8. Paul put this truth another way in verse 8. What did he say?

9. According to verses 9–12, who will be our judge at the end of time?

10. What two commands are given in verse 13?

These verses offer more words of caution about judging as well as placing a stumbling block before a fellow believer who may be offended by our choices. For example, if you feel free to drink wine or watch movies that you know would offend your sister in Christ, then out of love you should abstain from both activities when you're with her.

When is an issue considered disputable? In general, if the issue isn't completely clear in Scripture and doesn't have to do with the core tenets of Christianity (who Jesus is, why

He came, and how we are saved), then it's probably disputable.

11. What disputable issues cause conflict among believers today?

12. In light of Romans 14, how do you think the Lord would have you respond to a sister who believes differently than you do about one of these issues?

Detective for the Divine

In what ways have you grown in your love for God in the past twenty-four hours?

DAY 2

Pacifism Versus the "Just War" Theory

One example of a disputable matter that is relevant to our discussion at the close of Esther is to consider how God would have our government handle conflict. This is the issue Esther, as queen of Persia, and Mordecai faced. The edict has gone out; all the Jews are to be attacked on a single day. What are they to do?

Many scholarly books have been written by believers who are pacifists and also by believers who subscribe to the "Just War" theory. Certainly, since we will have to give an account of ourselves to God, it would be wise to consider this issue seriously, going beyond the brief summary I will give for each position. First let's begin with the pacifist view.

Pacifism. It's important to understand that pacifists don't suggest that we do nothing in the face of evil, but rather, they believe in alternative ways of overcoming evil with good. Esther herself demonstrated a nonviolent approach when she fasted and prayed before going to Xerxes. We also have many other great historical figures who overcame great evil through nonviolent methods: Mahatma Gandhi, Martin Luther King Jr., President Jimmy Carter, and countless more. Many missionaries have laid down their lives, refusing to respond to violence with violence, and their martyrdom was indeed an expression of faith that was followed by much fruit: the conversion of unbelievers and the strengthening of believers. Pacifism is often much more effective in bearing fruit than the cycle of violence.

13. What peaceful solution to conflict did Esther propose in Esther 4:15–16?

14. What peaceful solutions to overcoming violence stand out to you in history?

"Just War" theory. Those who believe that war is a legitimate and godly response in some situations would also subscribe to principles that differentiate a just war from an unjust war. As with all conflict, either between individuals or nations, we can only choose for ourselves. Proverbs 16:7 says, "When a man's ways please the LORD, he makes even his enemies live at peace with him." Though a nation such as ours may neither revere God or Scripture, they may still discover that a subscribing to a just war is pragmatic and expeditious, whereas unjust measures are more likely to perpetuate the cycle of violence.[2] Here is thinker Daniel Buttrey's set of principles for waging a just war:

1. A just war can only be waged as a last resort. All nonviolent options must be exhausted before the use of force can be justified.

2. A war is just only if it's waged by a legitimate authority. Even just causes cannot be served by actions taken by individuals or groups who don't constitute an authority sanctioned by whatever the society and outsiders to the society deem legitimate.

3. A just war can only be fought to redress a wrong suffered. For example, self-defense against an armed attack is always considered to be a just cause, although the justice of the cause isn't sufficient (see point 4). Furthermore, a just war can only be fought with "right" intentions: The only permissible objective of a just war is to redress the injury.

4. A war can only be just if it's fought with a reasonable chance of success. Deaths and injury incurred in a hopeless cause are not morally justifiable.

5. The ultimate goal of a just war is to reestablish peace. More specifically, the peace established after the war must be preferable to the peace that would have prevailed if the war hadn't been fought.

6. The violence used in the war must be proportional to the injury suffered. States are prohibited from using force not necessary to attain the limited objective of addressing the injury suffered.

7. The weapons used in war must discriminate between combatants and noncombatants. Civilians are never permissible targets of war, and every effort must be taken to avoid killing civilians. The deaths of civilians are justified only if they are unavoidable victims of a deliberate attack on a military target.[3]

In the Old Testament, wars were commanded or condemned by God. In Esther, however, He is silent.

Read 1 Samuel 15.

15. Describe the conversation between Saul and Samuel that followed. (vv. 10–31)

Because Haman was a descendant of the Amalekites, many feel that Esther and Mordecai finished what Saul had failed to do. However, that can be a dangerous principle, for can we really know whether God was still commanding such a war generations later?

Sometimes it's expressly stated in the Old Testament that a war was of God (e.g., Deut. 4:33–35) and other times that it wasn't (e.g., Num. 14:39-45).

> 16. War became the habit of David's life, for every spring the men went out to war. What do you learn about this from 1 Chronicles 22:6–8?

Was the war at the close of Esther sanctioned by God or not? Some commentators point out that it wasn't unrestrained bloodshed, that the edict written by Esther and Mordecai on behalf of the king gave the Jews permission to defend themselves against anyone who "might" (in the sense of could/would/did) choose to attack them (Est. 8:11). The edict didn't give them permission to attack any enemy unprovoked. Commentators also point out that even though the edict gave them permission to plunder those who attacked them, the narrator of Esther repeatedly says that no plunder was taken. These commentators believe—and they may be right—that God was working through this decree to protect the Jews. That seems to be the purpose of the wars in the Old Testament.

Chuck Swindoll compares the closing in Esther to "giving concentration camp prisoners long-overdue rights."[4] That comparison helps us identify with the horror the Jews in Persia had been through and how glad they were to finally be able to protect themselves.

When you realize that the Jews waited a whole year for the anticipated holocaust, it's logical that they might have been able to discover genuine enemies during that time. Perhaps God arranged the timing that way so that those with malevolent intentions would reveal themselves. (Can't you imagine it? A prejudiced Persian tells a Jewish family, "I'm going to get you on that day.") This turning of the tables, causing the enemies of the Jews to fall into their own trap would be consistent with the pattern we have seen in Esther and in the didactic scriptures. (See, for example, Proverbs 1:10–19.) God may, in fact, have planned the slaughter at the close of Esther.

On the other hand, others are deeply offended by the slaughter of seventy-five thousand boys and men. Wives were mourning for their husbands, mothers wept for their sons, and children were bereft of their fathers. F. B. Huey Jr., in *The Expositor's Commentary,* writes,

> The Jews did not limit themselves to self-defense. They hunted out and destroyed those who might harm them.... Could not Esther also be interpreted as another example of the postexilic failure of the Jewish people to become the exemplary people of God that he meant them to be?[5]

I've wondered why neither Mordecai nor Esther is mentioned in Hebrews 11, as so many of God's people were. They seem to fade out of the pages of Scripture. Is this significant or not? We may not learn the answer to this question until we see Jesus face-to-face. In fact, I doubt we'll discover the answers to most of the mysterious paradoxes of Scripture while we're on this earth. And in the absence of editorial commentary in Esther, we cannot know for certain whether the Jewish people went beyond God's will in protecting themselves to engaging in vengeance.

17. What does 1 Timothy 2:1–2 teach? How might you cultivate this habit?

Memory Work

Spend a few minutes working on perfecting your memory verses.

DAY 3
. . . .

The Royal Horses Raced Out

The laws of the Medes and Persians couldn't be changed. Frederic Bush writes that in Hebrew the use of the emphasizing particle Xerxes used in Esther 8:7 shows an exasperated tone: "Look at what I have done for you! I have hanged Haman and given you his estate. What more do you want?"[6] Xerxes wasn't concerned with the slaughter of the Jews, but Esther's diplomacy had prevailed, and, giving in, Xerxes took off his signet ring and, in characteristic irresponsibility, gave Esther and Mordecai the power to do whatever they chose. I so admire Esther for her persistence and diplomacy. How we must pray for this for our leaders, so that needless bloodshed can be spared. Xerxes agrees—not because he has a heart of compassion, but because God has worked through his diplomatic and skillful wife. Esther helped Xerxes save face, being as gentle as a dove and as wise as a serpent.

Then Esther deferred to Mordecai, who wrote a new order, turning the tables. The Jews could assemble, protect themselves, and annihilate any armed force that might attack them. The couriers raced out on royal horses to post the new edict.

Read Esther 8:7–17.

18. What authority did Xerxes give Esther and Mordecai? (vv. 7–8)

19. Compare Esther 3:13–15 with Esther 8:9–10. What similarities do you see? What differences?

20. Describe the first part of the new edict (v. 11).

The Hebrew in verse 11 is difficult to interpret, and some commentators think it means that the Jews could kill women and children and take the plunder. But Joyce Baldwin believes that the use of the verb "attack" as it relates to "women and children" meant that the Jews could kill anyone who attacked their women and children and plundered their property.[7]

21. In addition to defending themselves, what else did the edict give the Jews permission to do? (v. 11b)

22. What does verse 13 say was the purpose of making the edict known in "every province" and to "every nationality"?

Many commentators feel that at this point Mordecai and Esther went beyond leading a just war in which defense was the primary motivation to waging a war of vengeance. F. B. Huey Jr. writes,

> If Esther and Mordecai had forgiven their enemies instead of demanding vengeance, would God have been pleased and protected his people? ...

> Could God's silence in Esther be interpreted as evidence that the people were working out their own affairs without consulting Him? There is no historical evidence that the Jewish people entered into a period of blessing after the events of Esther, a blessing that might have been expected if God were guiding their actions (Deut. 28).[8]

23. What reaction did many people from other nationalities have to the edict? (v. 17)

24. Why do you think they thought it would be advantageous to become Jewish? Do you think they were sincere converts to Judaism? Explain.

Read Esther 9:1–17.

25. Describe what happened on the first day the tables were turned. (vv. 1–10)

26. What else did Esther request of the king? (vv. 11–13)

27. Describe what happened on the second day of the conflict. (vv. 14–17)

28. What do you think about the measures the Jews took to gain "relief" from their enemies (Est. 9:22)? Does it sound to you like a "just war"? Explain your reasoning.

Detective for the Divine

In what ways have you seen God at work in your life in the past twenty-four hours?

DAY 4
. . . .

Mourning into a Day of Celebration

Mordecai and Esther established a day of celebration to commemorate the month "when their sorrow was turned into joy and their mourning into a day of celebration" (Esther 9:22). Frederic Bush points out that Purim is understood to be a reference to the pur, the lot cast by Haman. So "the very name of the festival itself brings to mind neither military victory nor the slaughter of enemies, but Haman's plot and [the Jewish people's] subsequent deliverance from evil and disaster."[9]

I can see Esther's hand in establishing the traditions for Purim. The day before Purim begins, orthodox Jews fast to commemorate Esther's fast. During the days of feasting with Purim, we see, again, that Jews give presents of food to one another and to the poor, just as happened in Esther 9:19, 22. Joyce Baldwin likens it to the child who comes back from a party with a choice morsel wrapped in a napkin for one who is special to him. Drawing upon research by Sandra Beth Berg, Baldwin illuminates a deeper meaning in this particular tradition. I think these two distinguished women are right, and to me their commentary illuminates not only the custom of sending portions to one another but also Esther's faith. So read the following description carefully!

In the King James Version, verse 19 is translated "portions one to another," and verse 22 is translated "sending portions one to another, and gifts to the poor," This same Hebrew word for "portion" is used in Psalm 16:5 when the Lord is called our "portion." Verse 6 goes on to say, "The lines are fallen unto me in pleasant places."

Read Esther 9:18—10:3.

29. According to 9:22, what was the purpose of Purim?

30. Why was it called Purim? (9:24)

31. What relationship do you see between the name "Purim" and God's providence?

32. In Esther 9:19, 22, the Jews were to send "portions" to one another. Have you observed the tradition of bringing home a "portion" from a party or a holiday event to a loved one? What message does that convey?

33. In Psalm 16:5–6, how is the word "portion" used? What do you think this means?

34. What evidence do you find in Esther 9:18–32 that God's favor was on Esther, that He made her "lot secure"?

35. What other tradition was established in 9:31? What would this bring to mind?

36. According to 9:27–28, how many days were set aside to celebrate Purim? How often was it to be celebrated and why?

37. How did God continue to protect His people in Persia? (10:3)

Frederic Bush points out that Hitler, unlike Haman, was successful in eliminating six million Jews. For those Jews, there was no Esther. He writes, "Faith hardly knows how to hang on to the providence of God in such circumstances—but it must."[10] For this reason, Bush reflects, the book of Esther and the celebration of Purim become especially important, summoning the community to hold on to its faith and its hope.[11]

38. Have you ever experienced a time in your life when you struggled to "hang on to the providence of God" in the midst of difficult circumstances in which He was silent? If so, briefly describe how you felt and what helped you hold on to your faith and hope.

As I was writing this guide, a birth announcement arrived from missionary friends, Travis and Susan Stewart, who years ago suffered the death of their long-awaited and only child, a newborn boy. On the birth announcement was a picture of their daughter, Laura Joy, and a verse from the book of Esther: "Sorrow was turned into joy and their mourning into a day of celebration" (9:22).

39. Share a time, if any, when God turned your sorrow into joy.

40. When life is difficult for you, what evidence can you look back on that reminds you of God's love and care?

Memory Work

Review your memory verses.

DAY 5

. . . .

Celebrations That Honor God

Purim is still observed by many of the Jewish faith. Every year a festival is held in the streets of Tel Aviv and is attended by thousands. In keeping with the satirical spirit of Esther, there is little decorum and much merriment, somewhat like Halloween or New Year's Eve. Children wear costumes and have their faces painted, and when the book of Esther is read aloud, they blow noisemakers every time they hear Haman's name and cheer when they hear the names of Mordecai and Esther. People send portions of food to their friends—the most popular portions are three-cornered pies called "Haman's pockets."[12] Three prayers are also offered during Purim in which the Jews thank Jehovah for preserving their ancestors and for granting them another year of life to celebrate the festival again.[13]

Purim was established not by God but by Mordecai and Esther, yet that doesn't mean it can't be honoring to Him. It can be a time when people reflect on the reality of God and His care, or it can simply be a time to eat, drink, and be merry. Likewise, Thanksgiving, Christmas, and Easter were established by believers, not God, and yet these celebrations can honor Him. However, for many people, they have become simply times to eat, drink, and be merry.

Holiday traditions can teach our children about God. The high point of our Thanksgiving occurs when each person at the table gives thanks for something he or she could not have been thankful for the previous year. Christmas carols are filled with essential Christian doctrines, and we should be singing them together in our cars and in our homes. Fasting on Good Friday or giving up something during Lent can be a reminder of what Christ gave up for us. Likewise, Easter baskets laden with jelly beans can remind us of God's goodness. (This tradition reminds me of the fast before Purim and then the feast of Purim.) However, traditions can easily be passed on without their meaning—a form of godliness without the power (see 2 Tim. 3:5). The real secret to meaningful holidays is getting our hearts right with God. The rest will follow, for the way we celebrate is a reflection of our hearts.

41. Think about some recent holiday celebrations with your family. How did those times reflect your passion (or lack of passion) for God?

Read Nehemiah 8:5–12.

Nehemiah is a story of revival, and Ezra was the priest who led the revival. The people wept in repentance as Ezra read from God's Word. Then Nehemiah led them in a celebration that's similar to the celebration we see described at the end of Esther.

42. What instructions did Nehemiah and the Levite priests give to the people? (vv. 9–12)

43. What similarities do you see between this celebration and the celebration of Purim in Esther 9?

44. What similarities do you see between the celebrations in Nehemiah or Esther and our celebrations of Thanksgiving, Christmas, and Easter?

Read Isaiah 1:10–20.

45. Why did God hate the festivals and celebrations of the Israelites?

46. What did He long to see in their lives?

Read Isaiah 58.

47. Why was God not pleased with the fasts of the Israelites?

48. What did He long to see in their lives?

Memory Work

Repeat your memory verses aloud a few times until you can say them without making any mistakes. (Make sure to include Romans 11:33–36.)

Detective for the Divine

How have you seen God at work in your life in the past twenty-four hours through His Word, His presence, and His provision?

What was your most meaningful "Detective for the Divine" discovery this week? How can you apply this to your life?

Prayer Time

Pair off in twos and pray together. Spend some time praying for your government leaders and others in positions of authority.

Nine

Review

Although the events in the book of Esther occurred more than twenty-five centuries ago, the struggles against sin and Satan sound just like the struggles of our day. We live in a world that is filled with pride and prejudice, vanity and violence. Many of our leaders, and even those who call themselves believers, are obsessed with sexual immorality, entertainment, materialism, and vengeance. Yet God seems strangely silent.

We live in a world that's in desperate need of spiritual revival. But before worldwide revival can take place, it must first begin with each of us. The book of Esther gives us the opportunity to reflect on the state of our own hearts so that God can in turn work through us to bring revival to the world around us.

Prepare Your Heart to Hear

Ask God to remind you each day of something He showed you or impressed on your heart during the past eight weeks of this study.

Memory Work

Spend some time meditating on the passages you committed to memory over the past eight weeks:

> *Oh, the depth of the riches of the wisdom and knowledge of God! How unsearchable his judgments, and his paths beyond tracing out!*
>
> *"Who has known the mind of the Lord? Or who has been his counselor?"*
>
> *"Who has ever given to God, that God should repay him?"*
>
> *For from him and through him and to him are all things.*
>
> *To him be the glory forever! Amen.* (Rom. 11:33–36)

When Esther's words were reported to Mordecai, he sent back this answer: "Do not think that because you are in the king's house you alone of all the Jews will escape. For if you remain silent at this time, relief and deliverance for the Jews will arise from another place, but you and your father's family will perish. And who knows but that you have come to this royal position for such a time as this?"

Then Esther sent this reply to Mordecai: "Go, gather together all the Jews who are in Susa, and fast for me. Do not eat or drink for three days, night or day. I and my maids will fast as you do. When this is done, I will go to the king, even though it is against the law. And if I perish, I perish. (Est. 4:12–16)

WARMUP

In a year, what do you think you'll remember about the book of Esther that will continue to have an impact on your life?

DAY I
· ·

"He Is There and He Is Not Silent"

Perhaps the strongest theme in the book of Esther is that God is in control, working behind the scenes. Reflect on this theme as you answer the following questions.

1. Complete the following statement and spend a few moments pondering what it means to you: The God of Esther is the God of _____ (fill in your name). Write any thoughts you may have.

2. Skim the book of Esther and write down any evidence of God working behind the scenes, caring for His children, bringing beauty out of ashes.

3. Review the story of Daniel and his friends (Daniel 1; 3) and contrast them with Esther and Mordecai. What do you see? What have you learned about how to view the heroes of Scripture?

Detective for the Divine

How have you seen God at work in your life this week through His Word?

DAY 2

The Party and the Contest

Satire is thick in the book of Esther, pointing out the folly of humans and their grandiose schemes. As Dallas Willard described it in *The Divine Conspiracy*, they are "flying upside down," like a disoriented airplane pilot who thinks he's flying toward the sky, because it feels as if he is, but in reality, he's flying toward the ground to his death.[1] Likewise, in our folly and self-deception, we can easily end up "flying upside down," plunging toward our death, if we aren't immersed in God's Word.

4. What elements of satire in Esther 1 did you find most interesting? Explain.

5. Review the contest for the new Miss Persia (Esther 2) and describe any elements of satire you find.

6. What have you learned from Esther about the things we allow to define us (e.g., our appearance, our ability to please others, etc.)? What do you think defines you?

   What Scriptures speak to your heart about this issue and can help you define yourself according to God's truth? (Possibilities: Proverbs 31:30 and 1 Samuel 16:7)

7. If you or someone you love has been a victim of sexual abuse, what comfort can you find from Esther's story?

Memory Work

Spend some time reviewing your memory verses for this study.

DAY 3

Predicament, Privilege, and Providence

Often it's during our most painful times in life that the most growth occurs. I so wanted to protect my children from losing their father, and yet I have seen that though they live with tremendous loss and pain, their souls are also being enlarged. Because they trust God, He is sanctifying them in their distress, that is, He is making them stronger, holier, and more compassionate people. Even though the Jews in Esther experienced great darkness and despair, God truly was in control and turned ashes into beauty.

Songs of Praise

Begin your quiet time by singing "Immortal, Invisible" and "In His Time."

8. Reflect on the predicament of the Jews at the beginning of Esther 4 and record your thoughts about how they responded to their situation. What made the greatest impression on you? Why?

9. What did you learn from Esther's example about how privilege can be used for good?

10. Give an example of someone in modern times who used their privilege for good. How can you use your own God-given privilege (your influence, talents, abilities, etc.) to help others?

11. Review Esther 4:12–14 and make at least five observations from the text. Then share at least two applications to your life.

Detective for the Divine

How have you seen God's presence and provision in your life this week?

DAY 4

. . . .

Influencing Men and Experiencing God

Whether you're dealing with a difficult boss, approaching a husband who is about to make a mistake, or battling spiritual enemies in high places, Esther has much to teach us about experiencing the power of God in the midst of difficult circumstances.

12. What did you learn about fasting from Scripture and from Esther's example?

13. What did you learn from the positive examples of Esther, Abigail, and Sarah about how to approach your husband (or someone in authority) when you think he's about to make a serious mistake?

14. Review the negative example of Haman's wife, Zeresh, and describe a time, if any, when you responded to your husband (or someone in authority) in a foolish or dangerous way. What did you learn from this experience?

Memory Work

Spend some time perfecting your memory verses for this study.

DAY 5

. . . .

Sorrow into Joy

In His time, God will always turn sorrow into joy and mourning into dancing. He also promises us that He will right the tables of injustice. Sometimes we won't see this happen until glory, but now and then He lets us taste it right here on earth. He certainly did that for His people in the book of Esther, and they established a lasting celebration to remember His care.

15. Describe a time, if any, when God brought beauty out of ashes in your life and turned your mourning to dancing. In what ways did this experience strengthen your faith in Him?

16. What are your final thoughts about the war at the close of the story?

When, if ever, have you been tempted to seek vengeance for some injustice in your own life? What perspective did you gain from Jesus' example in the face of unjust treatment? (Review 1 Peter 2:21–23.)

17. What did you learn from the story of Esther about the importance of celebrating God's providence and protection?

What aspects of the Jewish celebration of Purim were most meaningful to you? Do you think you might be able to incorporate any of these aspects into your own celebrations? Explain.

18. What did you learn from Esther about being a woman of faith? How will you apply this to your life?

Memory Work

Review the memory verses for this study (Romans 11:33 and Esther 4:12–16) and write them out below from memory.

Detective for the Divine

Skim through each of your Detective for the Divine moments in this study guide and list the three most memorable ones. Why were they memorable for you?

Prayer Time

Based on what you shared about becoming a woman of faith, pray for one another, asking God to etch this truth in your heart so that your life will be transformed.

Leader's Helps

CHAPTER ONE

STRANGERS ON EARTH

Question 6. 1 Corinthians 3:11 makes it clear that "no one can lay any foundation other" than Jesus. So it is Peter's profession of faith in the Christ rather than Peter himself.

Question 15. Be willing to lead the way, modeling vulnerability and brevity.

CHAPTER TWO

THE PURPOSE OF OUR JOURNEY

Question 8. God the Father elected believers, God the Spirit sanctified them, and God the Son died for them.

Question 11. Our part is faith (though even faith is a gift from God) and His part is to keep us through His power.

CHAPTER THREE

PRECIOUS, CHOSEN, AND BELOVED

Question 3. Malice: harboring evil intent toward someone
  Deceit: a subtle form of lying, where you tell a partial truth or withhold truth
  Hypocrisy: saying one thing, doing another
  Envy: Wanting what belongs to another
  Slander: Telling untruths about another, defaming their character

Question 23C. Looking back, first, was disobedient—because they had been told not to look back. Secondly, it showed symbolically how she was longing for the old way of life instead of trusting God and moving on.

CHAPTER FOUR

UNDERSTANDING SUBMISSION IN THE LIGHT OF 1 PETER

Question 21. 1 Peter 3:1 is a pun, not to be pressed too precisely. The fact that we are to be ready to give an answer in 1 Peter 3:15 shows wives should answer their husband's questions in an attitude of humility. The emphasis seems to be that our lives will be so filled with the power of Christ that it will provoke curiosity. Each situation requires sensitivity to the Spirit, for there is a time to speak and a time to be silent.

CHAPTER FIVE

WINSOME, WINNING WOMEN

Question 7. The phrase translated "not bound" is very strong–it truly means set completely free. Of what is she or he set free? She is not bound any longer to the covenant she made, she is set free to marry another. However, if she drives the unbeliever out, God will hold her accountable for that, for He is not mocked. God is holy, but He is also merciful. His heart breaks for the victim that has been abandoned, and truly, He gives her His blessing for a new beginning.

Question 12. A woman should not be afraid to set boundaries when her husband is requesting immoral behavior. She can say, "I love you, but before God I cannot: lie to your boss and say you are sick when you are not; cheat on our income tax; have an abortion; watch pornographic movies…"

Question 21. It is important that she see herself as a coheir rather than one of her husband's children. She should pray, research, and seek God—and then gently submit any wisdom she has. She should not give orders or nag.

CHAPTER SIX

THE HIDDEN PERSON OF THE HEART

Question 13. Sarah asked Abraham to sleep with her maidservant, Hagar, so that "I can build a family through her." We can be empathetic with Sarah's choice–for this practice was accepted in this culture and God had not yet made it clear that the promised child would come not only from Abraham, but also from Sarah. Yet God never leads into sin–never asks us to make "a deal with the devil to get over the bridge." The Spirit of God would not have given Sarah peace about this–it was a move that lacked faith and led to all kinds of heartache, not only for this family, but for generations to come. Even if a practice is accepted in our culture, we have a responsibility to be still before God, and to obey only Him.

Question 15. Examples of Sarah's faith:

A. Genesis 12:1–5

Not only Abraham but Sarah left her country, her people, and her father's house and went to an unknown land.

B. Genesis 13:7–18

Abraham gave Lot first choice of the land—Sarah had to trust God that this would work out for their best.

C. Genesis 18:1–6

Abraham knew he could ask her to help prepare a large meal quickly and she would cooperate wholeheartedly. That kind of response often comes from faith that God is leading your husband.

D. Genesis 22:1–19

If Sarah knew what Abraham was planning to do, this too required faith on her part.

Question 27. She could pray for God to help him overcome his fears, she could affirm when he does, she could model vulnerable sharing, and she could resist nagging.

CHAPTER SEVEN
SET APART CHRIST IN YOUR HEART AS LORD

Question 14. A sacrament cannot save. Only Christ can save. Our faith is only as reliable as the object in which it is placed.

CHAPTER EIGHT
CALLED TO HIS ETERNAL GLORY

Be sure to leave at least half of your time for the last four questions in the guide. Go around with at least two of these, giving women the freedom to pass.

Hymns Index

Immortal, Invisible, God Only Wise

Now to the King eternal, immortal, invisible, the only God, be honor and glory for ever.
1 Timothy 1:17

> 1. Im - mor - tal, in - vis - i - ble, God on - ly wise,
> 2. Un - rest - ing, un - hast - ing, and si - lent as light,
> 3. To all, life Thou giv - est— to both great and small;
> 4. Great Fa - ther of glo - ry, pure Fa - ther of light,

In light in - ac - ces - si - ble hid from our eyes,
Nor want - ing, nor wast - ing, Thou rul - est in might;
In all life Thou liv - est— the true Life of all.
Thine an - gels a - dore Thee, all veil - ing their sight.

Most bless - ed, most glo - rious, the An - cient of Days,
Thy jus - tice, like moun - tains, high soar - ing a - bove
Thy wis - dom so bound - less, Thy mer - cy so free,
All laud we would ren - der— O help us to see

Al - might - y, vic - to - rious— Thy great name we praise.
Thy clouds, which are foun - tains of good - ness and love.
E - ter - nal Thy good - ness, for naught chang - eth Thee.
'Tis on - ly the splen - dor of light hid - eth Thee.

WORDS: Walter Chalmers Smith, 1867
MUSIC: Welsh Hymn Tune, 1839; harm. by John Roberts, 1839

ST. DENIO
11.11.11.11.

Great Is Thy Faithfulness

His compassions never fail. They are new every morning. Lamentations 3:22-23

1. Great is Thy faith - ful - ness, O God, my Fa - ther; There is no shad - ow of turn - ing with Thee. Thou chang - est not; Thy com - pas - sions, they fail not. As Thou hast been Thou for - ev - er wilt be.

2. Sum - mer and win - ter, and spring - time and har - vest, Sun, moon, and stars in their cours - es a - bove, Join with all na - ture in man - i - fold wit - ness To Thy great faith - ful - ness, mer - cy, and love.

3. Par - don for sin and a peace that en - dur - eth, Thy own dear pres - ence to cheer and to guide, Strength for to - day and bright hope for to - mor - row— Bless - ings all mine, with ten thou - sand be - side!

WORDS: Thomas O. Chisholm, 1923
MUSIC: William M. Runyan, 1923

FAITHFULNESS
11.10.11.10. w. Ref.

And Can It Be?

Christ Jesus came into the world to save sinners– of whom I am the worst.
1 Timothy 1:15

1. And can it be that I should gain An in - t'rest
2. He left His Fa - ther's throne a - bove, So free, so
3. Long my im - pris - oned spir - it lay, Fast bound in
4. No con - dem - na - tion now I dread; Je - sus, and

in the Sav - ior's blood? Died He for me, who caused His
in - fi - nite His grace! Emp - tied Him - self of all but
sin and na - ture's night. Thine eye dif - fused a quick - 'ning
all in Him, is mine! A - live in Him, my liv - ing

pain? For me who Him to death pur - sued? A - maz - ing
love, And bled for Ad - am's help - less race. 'Tis mer - cy
ray. I woke; the dun - geon flamed with light! My chains fell
Head, And clothed in righ - teous - ness di - vine, Bold I ap -

WORDS: Charles Wesley, 1738
MUSIC: Thomas Campbell, 1825

SAGINA
8.8.8.8.8.8. w. Ref.

love! how can it be That Thou, my God, shouldst
all, im-mense and free, For, O my God, it
off; my heart was free. I rose, went forth, and
proach th'e-ter-nal throne And claim the crown, thro'

Refrain

die for me? A-maz-ing love! how can it
found out me! 'Tis mer-cy all, im-mense and
fol-lowed Thee. My chains fell off; my heart was
Christ, my own. Bold I ap-proach th'e-ter-nal

1. A - maz-ing love! how
2. 'Tis mer-cy all, im -
3. My chains fell off; my
4. Bold I ap-proach th'e -

be That Thou, my God, shouldst die for me?
free, For, O my God, it found out me!
free. I rose, went forth, and fol-lowed Thee.
throne And claim the crown, thro' Christ, my own.

can it be That Thou, my God, shouldst die for me?
mense and free, For, O my God, it found out me!
heart was free. I rose, went forth, and fol-lowed Thee.
ter-nal throne And claim the crown, thro' Christ, my own.

End of Worship Sequence "AMAZING LOVE"

117

Amazing Grace

One thing I do know. I was blind but now I see! John 9:25

1. A - maz - ing grace! how sweet the sound That
2. 'Twas grace that taught my heart to fear, And
3. The Lord has prom - ised good to me; His
4. Thro' man - y dan - gers, toils, and snares I
5. When we've been there ten thou - sand years, Bright,

saved a wretch like me! I once was lost, but
grace my fears re - lieved. How pre - cious did that
word my hope se - cures. He will my shield and
have al - read - y come. 'Tis grace hath bro't me
shin - ing as the sun, We've no less days to

now am found; Was blind, but now I see.
grace ap - pear The hour I first be - lieved!
por - tion be As long as life en - dures.
safe thus far, And grace will lead me home.
sing God's praise Than when we'd first be - gun.

WORDS: John Newton, 1779; stanza 5, anonymous
MUSIC: *Virginia Harmony*, 1831; arr. by Edwin O. Excell, 1900

AMAZING GRACE
C.M.

End of Worship Sequence "GOD'S GREAT GRACE"

Memory Verses

WEEK 1

Oh, the depth of the riches of the wisdom and knowledge of God! How unsearchable His judgments, and His paths beyond tracing out! How unsearchable his judgments, and his paths beyond tracing out!

"Who has known the mind of the Lord? Or who has been his counselor?"

"Who has ever given to God, that God should repay him?"

For from him and through him and to him are all things. To him be the glory forever! Amen. (Rom. 11:33–36)

WEEKS 2–4

When Esther's words were reported to Mordecai, he sent back this answer: "Do not think that because you are in the king's house you alone of all the Jews will escape. For if you remain silent at this time, relief and deliverance for the Jews will arise from another place, but you and your father's family will perish. And who knows but that you have come to royal position for such a time as this?" (Est. 4:12–14)

WEEKS 5–8

Then Esther sent this reply to Mordecai: "Go, gather together all the Jews who are in Susa, and fast for me. Do not eat or drink for three days, night or day. I and my maids will fast as you do. When this is done, I will go to the king, even though it is against the law. And if I perish, I perish." (Est. 4:15–16)

Leader's Helps

Your Role:
A Facilitator for the Holy Spirit and an Encourager

A Facilitator for the Holy Spirit

People remember best what they articulate themselves, so your role as facilitator is to encourage discussion and keep it on track. Here are some things you can do to help:

1. Ask questions and allow silences until someone speaks up. If the silence seems interminable, rephrase the question, but don't answer it yourself!

2. Direct group members to look in the Scriptures for their answers. Ask, "Where in this passage can you find help for answering this question?"

3. Place chairs in as small a circle as possible. Too much space inhibits sharing.

4. Deal with the monopolizer:

   A. Pray for her control and ask God to help you find ways to make her feel valued, because excessive talking often springs from deep emotional needs.

   B. Wait for her to take a breath and gently say, "Thanks, could we hear from someone else now?"

   C. Go around the room with a question, giving people freedom to pass.

   D. Set down some ground rules at the beginning of the session. You can tell the group that you would like to hear from everyone. If someone has already spoken several times, she should give others time to speak up. If it becomes evident that this is a persistent problem, pass out three pennies to each member, telling them, "Each time you speak, you spend a penny. When they're gone, give the others a chance to spend theirs."

   E. So often in the Christian community we fail to speak the truth in love. Either we're silent and let problems destroy our relationships, or if we do speak, we aren't direct and loving. If you have a monopolizer in your group, and nothing you've tried so far is resolving the problem, you have a responsibility as facilitator to take the monopolizer aside and speak the truth in love. You might say something like this: "You share easily, but some women are so shy. They may have some wonderful things to say, but they need silences to gather the courage to speak up. I need your help." You could also ask her for ideas on how to help. She may surprise you! Here are some ideas you might consider trying:

- Star two or three questions for her to answer.

- After she shares, she could say, "What does someone else think?"

- She could watch the shy women's faces, and if it seems as if they have a thought, she could ask them if they have anything to add.

- She could count to ten before she shares to see if someone else will speak up first

5. The Detective for the Divine and Memory Work exercises will be used mightily in your group members' lives. If they aren't doing these exercises, call a few of the women during the week and ask them to join with you in being good examples to the group. Soon the others will follow!

An Encourager

Most women who drop out of a group do so not because the study is too challenging, but because they don't feel valued. Here are some things you can do as a facilitator to help each woman feel valued:

1. Greet each woman warmly when she walks in the door. This meeting should be the high point of her week!

2. Affirm answers when you can genuinely do so—"Good insight!" "Great!" "Thank you!" And always affirm nonverbally with your eyes, a smile, a nod.

3. If a woman gives a wrong or off-the-wall answer, be careful not to crush her. You can still affirm her by saying, "That's interesting. What does someone else think?" If you feel her response must be corrected, someone in the group will probably do it. If they don't, space your correction so it doesn't immediately follow her response and isn't obviously directed at her.

4. If this is an interdenominational group, set this ground rule: No one is to speak unfavorably of another denomination.

5. Plan an evening, lunch, or breakfast just to get to know one another. Play games, have a time of blessing one another, or just chat. A ninety-minute movie on Esther that is quite true to the Scripture is available through Dee's Web site. Another possibility is to watch the director's commentary, in whole or in part, on the DVD of *Memoirs of a Geisha*. Both of these would lead to interesting and relevant discussions but you would need to allow at least three hours to also provide time for fellowship and discussion.

6. Send notes or e-mails as friendly reminders to women who don't attend regularly, and send postcards to faithful attendees to express your appreciation.

7. Teach the women to pray without sharing their prayer requests first. That way they'll not only have the time to pray, but they'll also have the experience of seeing God at work in their lives.

Leader's Helps for Week 1
"He Is There and He Is Not Silent"

Question 4C. Sin provokes God and brings harm to us.

Question 6. Esther, cousin of Mordecai; Mordecai, the son of Jair; Jair, the son of Shimei; Shimai, the son of Kish.

Question 19. Sometimes a Scripture passage provides direct editorial commentary on a character's actions, such as when David committed adultery. There are also instances where an Old Testament character is commended or condemned in a New Testament passage. For example, Cain is commented on negatively in 1 John, and many Old Testament heroes are commended in Hebrews 11. If there is no commentary, as in Esther, we need to compare the narrative to the didactic (teaching) scriptures and ask what these scriptures have to say about sex outside of marriage, about showing honor to government leaders, and about obeying an immoral request from an authority figure.

Leader's Helps for Week 2
"He Who Sits in the Heavens Laughs"

Question 1. Point out the difference between the extensive descriptions of his wealth, wine, and wife, and then the succinct description of her refusal. (How quickly his huge balloon of self-importance was deflated!)

Question 3. There are several words and phrases that indicate that Xerxes and his subjects may have thought of him as a god (e.g., "the splendor and glory of his majesty" [v. 4]). Ask for them to share a few of the descriptions of the length of the party, the splendor of the palace, and the abundance of the wine.

Question 7. Pave the way for honesty by making yourself vulnerable and sharing your own thoughts and experiences.

Question 12:

A. Verses 13–15: The names of the seven "wise" men, when read aloud, have comical sounds. They "understood the times" but we will see how foolish was their advice.

B. Verses 16–18: Great concern that their wives might also stand up against abuse!

C. Verses 19–20: As if a law could cause you to respect someone!

D. Verses 20–21: Imagine the royal horses racing out so that this ridiculous edict could be posted everywhere!

Question 15. Note the contrast between the extensive description of the king's banquet and the one verse allotted for the queen's banquet. Note how the queen is described and how nothing is mentioned about her wisdom or character. Help the women see the satire here, because it's an important indication of God's scorn for this treatment of women. He never intended for women to be "play things," paraded around as sexual objects. Making Vashti's refusal an issue of "obedience" over which horsemen rushed around the kingdom posting edicts in every province is ridiculous in the extreme. God scorns those who don't understand the dignity He has bestowed upon women. But instead of stating this outright in Esther, God has written a satire.

Question 19. Memucan was disrespecting Vashti by eliminating her title, and he was probably hoping that Xerxes would do the same.

Question 25. As a husband loves his wife sacrificially, he becomes a portrait of Jesus. As a wife honors her husband, she becomes a portrait of the bride of Christ, the church. As they work together harmoniously to glorify God, they become a portrait of Christ and His church working together harmoniously to glorify God.

Question 32:

A. Abigail was beautiful and intelligent; her husband was surly and mean.

B. The narrator makes sure we know everything David and his men did and how Nabal feigned ignorance of David's identity and kindness.

C. Find examples of Abigail's swiftness, wisdom, and generosity. Also note verse 24.

D. Find examples contrasting David's ability to hear and respond with Nabal's.

E. Nabal's death is a editorial commentary from the Lord.

Leader's Helps for Week 3
The Contest for the New Miss Persia

Question 19. She went to the king in the evening and returned in the morning.

Question 20. Concubines were not virgins. A virgin was a young girl who had never had sexual relations with a man; a concubine was a woman with whom the king had already had sexual relations, and once she lost her virginity to the king, she would live with the other concubines for the rest of her life, even if he never had sexual relations with her again. No other man would ever be allowed to touch her.

Leader's Helps for Week 4
His Plans Are Not to Harm Us

Question 29. Truth: The Jews have been scattered. Half-truth: They refused to obey the king's laws. In fact, they obeyed anything that didn't go directly against God. Bold-faced lie: It wasn't in the best interest of the king to tolerate the Jews. In fact, they were the apple of God's eye, and anyone who touched them would experience His wrath. Haman himself would experience this.

Leader's Helps for Week 5
Predicament, Privilege, and Providence

Question 10. Esther mentioned the king five times. The repetition seems to demonstrate her fear.

Leader's Helps for Week 6
Out of the Cocoon of Crisis Emerges a Butterfly

Question 14C. A few of the key principles we find in the examples of Esther, Abigail, and Sarah are (1) fasting for God's wisdom and guidance; (2) keeping a humble attitude when approaching our husbands or a person in authority; (3) honoring our husbands or a person in authority; (4) trusting God in the midst of the situation; and (5) being willing to take action to avert a crisis.

Question 14D. Each of the women communicated with their husbands differently. Abigail didn't attempt to reason with her husband. (Many proverbs warn us against reasoning with a fool.) Esther told her husband the problem, but she had to do so very carefully. Sarah was the only one who seemed to feel free to speak the truth in love directly to her husband.

Leader's Helps for Week 7
"If God Is for Us, Who Can Be Against Us?"

Question 24. Haman was hanged for allegedly molesting the queen. Consider Xerxes' history.

Question 28. Esther returns to the king to plead for the lives of her people.

Question 29. Just as Esther interceded for the lives of her people, we need to intercede for the lives of our loved ones.

Leader's Helps for Week 8
Sorrow into Joy

Question 11. Examples of disputable issues for believers: whether it's acceptable for Christians to drink alcohol, whether parents should homeschool their children or send them to public school, whether some styles of dress are unacceptable, whether the Bible mandates head coverings for women in all cultures in all time periods, whether women should be allowed to fill a pastoral role of any kind, when the tribulation will occur, what modes of baptism are scriptural, which movies or books are edifying, whether Christians should date or court, whether Christians should support or participate in war, whether it's acceptable to eat out or shop on Sundays, and more.

Sources

1. "He Is There and He Is Not Silent"

1. Francis Schaeffer, *He Is There and He Is Not Silent* (Wheaton, IL: Tyndale, 1972).

2. Merrill Unger, *Unger's Bible Dictionary* (Chicago: Moody, 1966), s.v. "Providence."

3. Corrie ten Boom, *The Hiding Place* (Old Tappan, NJ: Fleming, 1971), 176.

4. Billy Graham, *Just As I Am: The Autobiography of Billy Graham* (New York: HarperCollins, 1997), 24.

5. Joni Eareckson Tada, *Secret Strength: For Those Who Search* (Portland, OR: Multnomah, 1988), 162.

6. Matthew Henry, *Matthew Henry's Commentary* (Peabody, MA: Hendrickson, 1991), 4:446.

7. J. Vernon McGee, *Ezra, Nehemiah, and Esther* (Nashville: Thomas Nelson, 1991), 170.

8. Unger, *Unger's Bible Dictionary*, s.v. "Cyrus."

9. F. B. Huey Jr., "Esther," *The Expositor's Bible Commentary*, vol. 4, ed. Frank E. Gaebelein and Richard P. Polcyn (Grand Rapids: Zondervan, 1988).

10. John Brug, *People's Commentary Bible: Ezra Nehemiah Esther* (St. Louis: C.P.H., 1985), 155–156.

11. Edward Mote, "The Solid Rock," *Sing to the Lord* (Kansas City: Lillenas Publishing Company, 1993, public domain.

12. Huey, "Esther," 786.

2. "He Who Sits in the Heavens Laughs"

1. "A Magical Merger," *People*, February 7, 2005, 58–61

2. C. S. Lewis, *The Weight of Glory and Other Addresses* (Grand Rapids: Eerdmans, 1965), 1–2.

3. Herodotus, quoted in J. G. McConville, *Ezra, Nehemiah, and Esther* (Philadelphia: Westminster, 1985), 156.

4. Joyce G. Baldwin, *Esther: An Introduction and Commentary* (Downers Grove, IL: InterVarsity Press, 1984), 55–56.

5. Flavius Josephus, *The Antiquities of the Jews, in Josephus: Complete Works,* trans. William Whiston (Grand Rapids: Kregel, 1981), 237.

6. W. Dinwiddie, "The Book of Esther," *The Pulpit Commentary*, vol. 7, ed. H. D. Spence and Joseph S. Exell (Peabody, MA: Hendrickson, 1985), 29.

7. Joni Eareckson Tada, *When God Weeps: Why Our Sufferings Matter to the Almighty* (Grand Rapids: Zondervan, 1997), 41–45.

8. F. B. Huey Jr., "Esther." *The Expositor's Bible Commentary,* vol. 4, ed. Frank E. Gaebelein and Richard P. Polcyn (Grand Rapids: Zondervan, 1988), 799.

9. Ibid.

10. Woodrow Kroll, "Living Courageously in Difficult Times" (radio address, Back to the Bible, 1997).

11. Charles R. Swindoll, *Esther: A Woman of Strength and Dignity* (Nashville: Word, 1997), 27.

12. Henry Cloud and John Townsend, *Boundaries* (Grand Rapids: Zondervan, 1992), 161–62.

3. The Contest for the New Miss Persia

1. Frederic W. Bush, "Esther," *Word Biblical Commentary*, vol. 9, ed. David A. Hubbard, Glenn W. Barker, and John W. Watts (Dallas: Word, 1996).

2. W. Clarkson, *The Pulpit Commentary* (Peabody, MA: Hendrickson, 1985), 54.

3. It breaks my heart to think of the young girls who have been sold into the sex trade. Many are abused, are emaciated with HIV-AIDS and have babies with the same disease, and are powerless to escape their desperate situation. We cannot turn our eyes away and do nothing. How badly light is needed to penetrate the darkness. How we need those who will pray, give, and go to rescue the perishing. World Hope International is one group that does a mighty work to help these women. To find out what you can do to help, visit their Web site at www.worldhope.org.

4. Carolyn Custis James, *Lost Women of the Bible: Finding Strength and Significance Through Their Stories* (Grand Rapids: Zondervan, 2005), 147.

5. Joyce G. Baldwin, The New Bible Commentary, rev. ed., ed. D. G. Guthrie and J. A. Motyer (Grand Rapids: Eerdmans, 1970), 415.

6. *Memoirs of a Geisha*, directed by Rob Marshall, Columbia Pictures, 2005.

7. Flavius Josephus, "The Antiquities of the Jews" in Josephus: Complete Works, trans. William Whiston (Grand Rapids: Kregel, 1981), 238.

8. Paton, quoted in Joyce G. Baldwin, Esther: An Introduction and Commentary (Downers Grove, IL: InterVarsity Press, 1984), 66.

9. F. B. Huey Jr., "Esther," *The Expositor's Bible Commentary*, vol. 4, ed. Frank E. Gaebelein and Richard P. Polcyn (Grand Rapids: Zondervan, 1988), 804.

10. Bush, "Esther," *Word Biblical Commentary*.

11. Carl Armerding, *Esther: For Such a Time as This* (Chicago: Moody, 1955), 40.

12. J. Vernon McGee, *Ezra, Nehemiah, and Esther* (Nashville: Thomas Nelson, 1991), 190.

13. James, *Lost Women*, 142.

14. Baldwin, *The New Bible Commentary*, "Esther," 66.

15. Jamieson, Fausset, and Brown, quoted in Armerding, Esther.

16. Baldwin, Esther, 68.

17. Armerding, Esther, 24–25, 29.

18. Tommy Tenney, Hadassah: One Night with the King (Minneapolis: Bethany House, 2004), 177.

19. D. Rowlands, "The Book of Esther," *Pulpit Commentary*.

20. Bush, "Esther," 365.

21. Baldwin, *New Bible Commentary*, 67–68

22. Rowlands, "The Book of Esther," *Pulpit Commentary*.

23. Charles Spurgeon, "Providence as Seen in the Book of Esther" (sermon, Metropolitan Tabernacle, Newington, November 1, 1874). Ages Digital CD-ROM.

4. His Plans Are Not to Harm Us

1. Woodrow Kroll, "Living Courageously in Difficult Days" (radio address, Back to the Bible, 1997).

2. Frederic W. Bush, "Esther," *Word Biblical Commentary*, vol. 9, ed. David A. Hubbard, Glenn W. Barker, and John W. Watts (Dallas: Word, 1996), 379.

3. Brennan Manning, *The Ragamuffin Gospel: Embracing the Unconditional Love of God* (Sisters, OR: Multnomah, 1990), 122.

4. Ibid., 130.

5. Bush, "Esther," 384.

6. John Walvoord and Roy Zuck, *The Bible Knowledge Commentary* (Colorado Springs: Cook, 1983), 705.

7. John C. Whitcomb, *Esther: Triumph of God's Sovereignty* (Chicago: Moody, 1979), 66.

8. Ibid.

5. Predicament, Privilege, and Providence

1. Joyce G. Baldwin, *Esther: An Introduction and Commentary* (Downers Grove, IL: InterVarsity Press, 1984), 76.

2. Frederic W. Bush, "Esther," *Word Biblical Commentary*, vol. 9, ed. David A. Hubbard, Glenn W. Barker, and John W. Watts (Dallas: Word, 1996), 398.

3. Baldwin, *Esther*, 77.

4. Gordon MacDonald quoted in Elizabeth Dole, "Crisis and Faith," *Finding God at Harvard: Spiritual Journeys of Thinking Christians*, ed. Kelly Monroe (Grand Rapids. Zondervan, 1996).

5. Ibid., 241.

6. Ibid., 242.

7. Baldwin, *Esther*, 76.

8. Charles R. Swindoll, Esther: A Woman of Strength and Dignity (Nashville: Word, 1997), 4.

9. Ibid.

6. Out of the Cocoon of Crisis Emerges a Butterfly

1. Sandra Glahn, *Espresso with Esther* (Colorado Springs: AMG Publishers, 2006), ix.

2. Woodrow Kroll, "Living Courageously During Difficult Days" (radio address, Back to the Bible, 1997).

3. Charles R. Swindoll, *Esther: A Woman of Strength and Dignity* (Nashville: Word, 1997), 96.

4. Brenda Wilbee, *Taming the Dragons: Christian Women Resolving Conflict* (New York: HarperSanFrancisco, 1992), 58.

5. David J. A. Clines, quoted in Frederic W. Bush, "Esther," *Word Biblical Commentary*, vol. 9, ed. David A. Hubbard, Glenn W. Barker, and John W. Watts (Dallas: Word, 1996), 407.

6. David Jeremiah "When A Wife Loves Her Husband II," *Turning Point,* (radio broadcast, June 14, 2006).

7. *"If God Is for Us, Who Can Be Against Us?"*

1. C. S. Lewis, *The Lion, the Witch and the Wardrobe* (New York: Collier Books, 1970), 103.

2. Ibid., 116, 118.

3. J. Vernon McGee, *Ezra, Nehemiah, and Esther* (Nashville: Thomas Nelson, 1991), 226.

4. Joyce G. Baldwin, *Esther: An Introduction and Commentary* (Downers Grove, IL: InterVarsity Press, 1984), 91.

5. David J. A. Clines, quoted in Frederic W. Bush, "Esther," Word Biblical Commentary, vol. 9, ed. David A. Hubbard, Glenn W. Barker, and John W. Watts (Dallas: Word, 1996), 433.

6. Joy Dawson, "Team Ministry" (speech, leadership conference, Seattle, Washington, March 1988).

8. *Sorrow into Joy*

1. R. C. Sproul, ed., *The Reformation Study Bible* (Nashville: Thomas Nelson, 1995), 1791.

2. Daniel L. Buttrey, *Christian Peacemaking* (Valley Forge, PA: Judson Press, 1984), 6–8.

3. Ibid.

4. Charles R. Swindoll, *Esther: A Woman of Strength and Dignity* (Nashville: Word, 1997), 158.

5. F. B. Huey Jr., "Esther." *The Expositor's Bible Commentary*, vol. 4, ed. Frank E. Gaebelein and Richard P. Polcyn (Grand Rapids: Zondervan, 1988), 787, 833.

6. Frederic W. Bush, "Esther," *Word Biblical Commentary*, vol. 9, ed. David A. Hubbard, Glenn W. Barker, and John W. Watts (Dallas: Word, 1996), 452.

7. Joyce G. Baldwin, *Esther: An Introduction and Commentary* (Downers Grove, IL: InterVarsity Press, 1984), 98.

8. Huey, "Esther," 787.

9. Bush, "Esther," 329.

10. Ibid. 331.

11. Ibid.

12. Ibid., 330.

13. J. Vernon McGee, *Ezra, Nehemiah, and Esther* (Nashville: Thomas Nelson, 1991), 246.

9. *Review*

1. Dallas Willard, *The Divine Conspiracy* (New York: HarperCollins, 1998).